FAITH, HOPE, AND CLARITY

FAITH, HOPE, AND CLARITY
Catholic Faith in Today's World

Pierre Riches

Lantern Books • New York
A Division of Booklight Inc.

2001
Lantern Books
One Union Square West, Suite 201
New York, NY 10003

Printed in the United States of America

Library of Congress Cataloging-in-Publication Data

Riches, Pierre
   [Note di catechismo per ignoranti colti. English]
   Faith, hope, and clarity : Catholic faith in today's world / Pierre Riches.
      p. cm.
   Originally pulbished: Back to basics. New York : Crossroad, 1984.
   Includes bibliographical references.
   ISBN 1-930051-53-0 (alk. paper)
 I. Catholic Church—Apologetic works. I. Title.

BX1752 .R4913 2001
230'.2—dc21
                                        2001038028

Contents

For J., J., Michael, F. and J.
in gratitude for love

The author thanks the Rothko Chapel for its help.

Preface

These notes are intended to be a simple, extremely simple, rough exposition of the reasoning (rational, intuitive and experiential) which has led me to accept Catholicism as the answer to the question "Has life any meaning?" (a question which I was already asking at the age of twelve).

My notes will take the form of short chapters, not always interrelated. Later (but who knows if or when?) I could extend each short chapter in various directions.

For the time being, I only want to provide more or less developed starting points for personal reflection. Each chapter should help the reader to clarify his ideas if he is asking himself the same questions I did. They should help him to build up his own 'world-view'.

Here I offer my own world-view, with its particular clarities and obscurities; each reader may stop where he wants, and then, perhaps, he will take an entirely different direction.

As chapter 35 says, there is 'a' truth, but it must be reached personally. No one can impose it and no individual can say: "This is the truth". He can only say: "There is a truth (and only one truth). My own reflections and experience of life tell me that truth can be defined in these terms rather than those, that it can be experienced in this way rather than that".

The evening before my baptism (I was 23 years old) my godfather asked me: "But do you really believe in it?" I replied: "If it's not true, it's certainly hangs together beautifully", and to this day I cannot say whether or not it is true, but I have not found anything that makes more sense, not even the Buddha.

PART I

The question and the answers

1

The question

There are not many possible answers to the question: "Has the world, has life itself any meaning?" There are only three answers: either "no" or "yes" or "perhaps, but we cannot know what it is".[1]

The way we live our lives will depend to a great extent on the answer we give to this question.

Now let us see a bit of the road along which each one of these answers would lead us:

If the answer is "no, life has no meaning", one can either despair and/or decide to "eat, drink and be merry for tomorrow we die".

We could also avoid thinking about it; we could live our own lives, filling each day with activity, but in bitterness because both reflection and hope would be excluded from our lives.

There are innumerable variations on this theme. Perhaps the most sophisticated is the totally egocentric view of life held by the libertine; a logical and practical consequence of this is despair, suicide, as the only way out.

To paraphrase one of Yeats' poems, *1919*: "Man is in love and loves what vanishes. What more is there to say?"

---

1. In strict logic, there would be others as well — for example:
"No, but we deceive ourselves into thinking it has" — and this comes back to my 'yes' (see chapter 35) — can we be deceived about the truth?
"Yes, but we shall never know what it is" — and this answer is included in my 'perhaps'.
"Yes, but it is incommunicable" — and then there is nothing more to say, and this 'yes' is Wittgenstein's "Whereof one cannot speak, thereof one must be silent".

2

The agnostic answer

If the answer is "perhaps, but we cannot know what it is", there are again many possibilities. One can simply remain agnostic and live one's life as best one can. There may be moments of great happiness but it seems to me that deep peace and serenity will be difficult to attain.

If we follow this path, truly seeking *how* to live, we will arrive at the same conclusions as the 'first' Buddha.

The Buddha, after a very sheltered childhood and youth in which he had never met old age, sickness or death, came upon these three scourges one day. His reaction was so strong that he decided to abandon everything and seek to liberate himself from their horror and terror.

After many years of searching among the various Indian philosophies of his time, and many years of penance and the most rigorous asceticism, he achieved enlightenment, and discovered that the source of all ills is desire and the attachment to the things which proceed from desire.

There are no answers to the basic questions of philosophy and what is more, even if there were any, they would be of no use. A very ancient Buddhist text illustrates this position very well:

"Bear always in mind what it is that I have not elucidated, and what it is that I have elucidated. And what have I not elucidated? I have not elucidated that the world is eternal; I have not elucidated that the world is not eternal; I have not elucidated that the world is finite; I have not elucidated that the world is infinite; I have not elucidated that the soul and body are identical; I have not elucidated that the monk who has attained (the arahat) exists after death; I have not elucidated that the arahat does not exist after death; I have not elucidated that the arahat both exists and does not exist after death; I have not elucidated that the arahat neither exists nor does not exist after death. And why have I not elucidated this? Because this profits not, nor has to do with the fundamentals of religion, therefore I have not elucidated this".

And what did the Buddha discover? What *is* of use? The next part of the same text tells us:

"And what have I elucidated? Misery have I elucidated; the origin of misery have I elucidated; the cessation of misery have I elucidated. And why have I elucidated this? Because this does profit, has to do with the fundamentals of religion, and tends to absence of passion, to knowledge, supreme wisdom, and Nirvana".[1]

So let us not ask ourselves what is true and what is not true; whether or not the world has any meaning, but let us detach ourselves from it, eliminating attachment and desire.

1. Majjhima Nikaya 63, in Henry Clarke Warren, *Buddhism in Translation*, Harvard University Press, 1922.

3

More about the Buddha

What the Buddha shows us is a life-style, a way, but not
knowledge. Two other early texts describe it to us.

The first is a legend:

> One day a grandmother appeared before him in
> tears. She had just lost a very dear grandchild. The
> Buddha looked at her gravely. "How many people are
> there in this city of Savatthi?" he asked, with apparent
> irrelevance. Upon receiving her reply, he came to the
> point: "Would you like to have as many children and
> grandchildren as there are people in Savatthi?" The
> old lady, still weeping, cried out yes, yes. "But", the
> Buddha gently remonstrated, "if you had as many
> children and grandchildren as there are people in
> Savatthi, you would weep every day, for people die
> daily there". The old lady thought a moment; he was
> right! As she went away comforted, she carried with
> her the Buddha's saying: "Those who have a hundred
> dear ones have a hundred woes; those who have ninety
> dear ones have ninety woes; . . . those who have one
> dear one have one woe; those who hold nothing dear
> have no woe".[1]

The second text is a long poem, *The Rhinoceros*. Here
are a few verses:

> Put by the rod for all that lives,
> Nor harm thou any one thereof;
> Long not for son — how then for friend?
> Fare lonely as rhinoceros.

Love cometh from companionship;
In wake of love upsurges ill;
Seeing the bane that comes of love,
    Fare lonely as rhinoceros.

Tangled as crowding bamboo boughs
Is fond regard for sons and wife:
As the tall tops are tangle-free,
    Fare lonely as rhinoceros.

In ruth for all his bosom-friends,
A man, heart-chained, neglects the goal:
Seeing this fear in fellowship,
    Fare lonely as rhinoceros.

Like lion fearful not of sounds,
Like wind not caught within a net,
Like lotus not by water soiled,
    Fare lonely as rhinoceros.

Folk serve and follow with an aim:
Friends who seek naught are scarce today:
Men, wise in selfish aims, are foul:
    Fare lonely as rhinoceros! [2]

We cannot know whether or not life has any meaning,
the Buddha tells us. Therefore let us not worry about knowing; let us rather seek a way of living free from pain and
suffering, let us detach ourselves from everything.

---

1. Udana VIII, 8, in James Bisset Pratt, *The Pilgrimage of Budd-hism*, Macmillan, 1928, p. 30.
2. Sutta Nipata 35-38, in *Buddhist Scriptures*, selected and tran-slated by Edward Conze, Penguin Books, 1959.

4

Other answers

We have spoken of how we can face a world with no meaning and also of how we can face a world which may or may not have a meaning but at best a meaning that we cannot understand, and in the second case we have proposed Buddha's solution as being the most coherent.

There is a third answer: the world has a meaning. This answer may be subdivided again and again and these subdivisions fall into two main groups:

1. *Either* life has a meaning in this world and only in this world (and one is therefore either an atheist or indifferent to the atheism-theism problem of whether or not God exists), and then the solutions will be of a politico-social nature or else purely individualistic. One person would opt, for example, for a Marxist or for a liberal political outlook and would seek to put it into practice; another would have his own personal view of temporal well-being for himself and/or his family and would strive to achieve it.

2. *Or* life has a meaning beyond this world; there is something which transcends the world and human nature and then the most coherent and satisfying answer seems to me to be the Catholic one.

I will not linger over the solutions which give life a meaning only in this world. (I confess that for someone of my temperament they seem unsatisfying, incomplete; by themselves they are non-solutions to the problem which interests me.) They are not discussed here, although many politico-social solutions deserve great respect and attention because they seek to answer real quetions which necessarily confront anyone who lives in this world.

5

Beyond this world — India

If on the other hand the meaning of life is to be found beyond this world, if there is something which transcends human nature, and we give the name 'God' to what is 'beyond' the world, to the thing which transcends human nature and 'explains' the world, then we are theists. There are very many kinds of theism. All types of theism, however, acknowledge that there is a force, a power, outside us.

There is general theism, then; more specifically, pantheism, dualism and, lastly, monotheism.

There are and always have been many general theists; these are the people who believe in a (vague) force, a (vague) Architect who is vaguely interested in men or completely uninterested in them. Pantheists are those who say that everything is God, everything is a divine manifestation and; finally, that nothing really exists that is not God.

The highest expression of this that I know is in Hinduism, wonderfully expressed in the *Chandogya Upanishad* (6, 12-13) with its repeated "Thou art that" (*Tat tvam asi*):

> "Bring me a fruit from this banyan tree".
> "Here it is, father".
> "Break it".
> "It is broken, Sir".
> "What do you see in it?"
> "Very small seeds, Sir".
> "Break one of them, my son".
> "It is broken, Sir".
> "What do you see in it?"
> "Nothing at all, Sir".

11

Then his father spoke to him: "My son, from the very essence in the seed which you cannot see comes in truth this vast banyan tree".

"Believe me, my son, an invisible and subtle essence is the Spirit of the whole universe. That is Reality. That is Atman. THOU ART THAT".

"Explain more to me, father", said Svetaketu.

"So be it, my son".

"Place this salt in water and come to me tomorrow morning".

Svetaketu did as he was commanded, and in the morning his father said to him: "Bring me the salt you put into the water last night".

Svetaketu looked into the water, but could not find it, for it had dissolved.

His father then said: "Taste the water from this side. How is it?"

"It is salt".

"Taste it from the middle. How is it?"

"It is salt".

"Taste it from that side. How is it?"

"It is salt".

"Look for the salt again and come again to me".

The son did so, saying: "I cannot see the salt. I only see the water".

His father then said: "In the same way, O my son, you cannot see the Spirit. But in truth he is here".

"An invisible and subtle essence is the Spirit of the whole universe. That is Reality. That is Truth. THOU ART THAT".[1]

There is very much more to be said on the subject of pantheism, which has many different meanings in different contexts, but for the moment it does not directly concern us.

1. *The Upanishads*, Penguin Classics, 1965, pp. 117-118.

6

Polytheism and monotheism

Polytheists believe in many gods; the Greek, Roman and Egyptian religions, among others, are examples of this. In their highest form they are close to pantheism and frequently rise above the simplistic materialism often attributed to polytheism.

Dualism affirms that there are two gods, one good and one evil. This form of religion took definite shape in Iran; from there it has influenced many other faiths.

Many more things of interest could be said about pantheism, polytheism and dualism; in some of their forms they represent a very fine and exalted expression of religious feeling.

Now let us turn to monotheism. This teaches that there is only one God.

Certain primitive religions are monotheistic but the best known monotheists are the followers of the so-called religions of 'the Book'.

The religions of the Book are Judaism and Christianity, whose 'Book' is the Bible, and Islam where the 'Book' is the Koran, which in its turn holds the Bible as sacred. Most men have adhered or adhere to one of these three great religions.

Historically it can be said that most people have believed in the transcendent, in God, in one or other of the many forms in which they believed they had found him. But in matters of belief, the majority is no authority. In the time of Galileo, the majority believed that the earth was immobile.

PART II

The Catholic position

7

God cannot be captured

Now I shall attempt an exposition which will help us to get our bearings in one of these positions: the Christian and, more precisely, the Catholic one.

The first thing to affirm is that if God exists, he cannot but be mysterious, he cannot but be unknowable, because by the term 'God' we are in fact referring to a being who transcends human nature and who is the source of and reason behind the universe.

God can never be known, God can never be understood, because God, if he exists, cannot but be 'greater' than the most powerful human intellect. He cannot be understood in the sense of being 'encompassed', 'captured', by our minds.

God is neither good, nor intelligent, nor omnipotent, nor omniscient, because goodness, power, intelligence and knowledge are human attributes and for this reason they can only be improperly applied to God.

However if we wish to speak about God we cannot but speak in human terms and so we use the words 'good', 'intelligent', etc. But the fact remains that *all* we say about God is inadequate and inaccurate.

If God exists he is in himself mysterious and unknowable. One cannot hope to know him, to pin him down, to possess him.

Any discussion of religion presupposes this fundamental assumption. Even if people often seem to be expressing certainties or making precise definitions, the presupposition is *always* that any description of God is inadequate.

8

Revelation

If God exists and is what we call 'good', he will be, among other things, open to encounters. Having created the universe from which human beings have developed, it is likely that he should want to make himself known in some way, to reveal himself, as we say, so that we may get to know him better.

And in fact during the course of man's history there are many experiences which point to revelation, which bear witness that God speaks.

The Catholic tradition divides them into two parts: natural and supernatural revelations.

In nature, God reveals himself either to our senses or to our reason: watching a marvellous sunset, a stormy sea, a mountain, one can easily sense the infinite, something 'beyond'. Writers and poets often tell of their inner experiences — one could also call them mystical experiences — which to them are signs of the infinite, a presence, a benign power, a creator.

A Christian often — not always — recognizes these indications, these feelings, as natural revelations of God.

God reveals himself to our reason as well. Aristotle, for example, concludes by reasoning that there must be an Unmoved Mover (*Metaphysics* XII, 6-9), and St Thomas Aquinas in his so-called Five Proofs of the Existence of God — which are not 'proofs' in the modern scientific sense, but, as he tells us, five ways of coming to God — lists the various ways in which reason can (should?) lead to the hypothesis of God, in response to the data of everyday life (*Summa Theologica*, Part 1, Q. 2, Art. 3).

These are philosophical ways — that of the Unmoved Mover, the First Cause, etc. — none of which seem to me to be proofs in themselves but, taken together, they increase the reasonable probability of the existence of God.

The First Vatican Council (Session III, ch. 2) goes as far as to state that man (*not* each single individual) can arrive in this way at certainty about the existence of God (Aristotle for example).

It is in all these ways that God reveals himself through nature. But there is another revelation which declares itself explicitly as such: this revelation is contained in the Bible and culminates in the person of Jesus of Nazareth.

9

The Bible

The Bible is a collection of writings by very different authors and editors, composed over a period which stretches from 1000 or more years before Christ to about 100 years after. Certainly they were not in written form at first but in an oral tradition handed down from generation to generation — as the Bedouin do to this day — and written down later. It is an extraordinarily beautiful book.

The Bible is divided into two main sections: the Old Testament and the New Testament. For the Jews, the Bible consists of the Old Testament only; for the Christian, it comprises both Testaments. Islam in its turn holds that the whole Bible is inspired by God, and the Koran uses it and is based upon it.

The books of the Old Testament are usually divided into three groups: the historical books, the prophetic books and the teaching or 'wisdom' books.

The historical books give us the history of the world from its beginning in the first eleven chapters of Genesis, then the story of Abraham and his descendants and finally the whole history of Israel until the second century before Christ.

The prophetic books are a collection of the sayings of the prophets. It should be noted that a prophet in Israel is not a person who specifically foretells the future, a seer, but one who speaks in God's name, acts as God's messenger and is usually rejected and persecuted. To be a prophet is a difficult task.

The teaching or wisdom books are books of poetry, proverbs, tales, songs (psalms) and writings that could be called philosophical.

So the Bible is a collection of books which differ very widely in their date of origin, style and subject matter; it is in fact the literature of a people, gathered together over many centuries.

One of the most striking things when one reads the Bible is to find that these books, despite their diversity, have the same vision of reality.

They have a *connecting thread* — a vision of God and his dealings with humanity — which really makes them into a unified work. The Bible gives human beings an important place in the universe, it makes them free and responsible, it gives meaning to their lives and this meaning is to be found only in the acknowledgement, fear (see chapter 67) and love of God. This vision is developed and extended through the various writings down the ages, but these fundamental points always remain the same.

There is no other literature which gives us such a unified and coherent interpretation of reality down the ages, and it is this fact which — humanly speaking — makes sense of the Church's affirmation that the Bible is the work of a single author: God.

10

The parts of the Bible

The first eleven chapters of Genesis (the first eleven chapters of the Bible) may be called mythical. They tell the story of the creation of the world — a story which may be found in various forms in every people and in nearly all religions — the story of the first human beings, Adam and Eve, of their disobedience, of their descendants Cain and Abel, of Noah and the universal flood and so on, up to the story of Abraham.

By saying that they are mythical I do not mean that they are untrue, mere legends or fables. I have in mind here the numerous theories and discoveries which have been made concerning myths by modern psychology and psychoanalysis. I will confine myself to explaining the way in which we are using the word 'myth' here. Often when human beings want to explain something very important or something which means a lot to them, they find themselves unable to do so in ordinary words, in prose, 'prosaically'. So they look for some other form of expression; the most obvious example is poetry. Certain feelings, certain sensations, can only be communicated in poetry. In a similar way, from the earliest times, people have used the form of the myth to express profound truths derived from human experience (the Oedipus myth, for example). The Genesis accounts are myths in this sense. They convey and communicate truths which can be conveyed only in this way and which make highly important statements about the human condition. We shall see this, for example, in the matter of original sin (see chapter 62).

From Abraham onwards, we can speak of real history,

although it is history as it used to be related well over twenty centuries ago, without the documentation which is such an important feature of history today. There is the story of Abraham and his son Isaac, Isaac's son Jacob, and then of the twelve sons of Jacob who formed the twelve tribes of Israel. The twelve go to Egypt and their descendants remain there for more than four hundred years. Towards 1250 B.C. comes the Exodus from Egypt to Palestine, led by Moses. The Exodus is the central event of Israel's history.

These facts are related in the first five books of the Bible, which also contain all the laws and precepts elaborated by the Hebrews of that period or inserted there from a later period. This is the Torah of the Hebrews, the Law of which Jesus speaks.

Then come other historical books: Joshua, Judges, Samuel, Kings, etc., which give an account of the settlement of the Hebrews in Palestine, their conquests, their unification, their transformation into a kingdom, the division into two kingdoms, those of Israel and Judah, their defeat by the Assyrians and Babylonians and the Deportation (721 B.C. for the Kingdom of Israel, 598-87 for the Kingdom of Judah), the return from exile by decree of Cyrus and so on until the revolt in the second century B.C. of the Maccabee brothers, Hebrew zealots, against the spread of Hellenism introduced by the successors of Alexander the Great.

The prophetic books, those of the so-called five 'major' and twelve 'minor' prophets, can be read alongside the historical books because they are mutually explanatory: the prophets very often refer to the historical events and the historical books frequently mention the prophets.

The teaching books, as we have seen, are each different and each has its own story and its own meaning. Their intellectual and literary standard is at times very high (for example, see chapter 37).

The New Testament can also be divided into three parts: the historical part consists of the four Gospels, that is, the life, death and resurrection of Jesus as told by Matthew, Mark, Luke and John; and the Acts of the Apostles which is the history of the early Church, above all the account of Peter's preaching and Paul's preaching and missionary journeys. The teaching part consists of the letters of the various apostles, twenty-one in all, thirteen of which are Paul's. They deal both with theological and practical problems. Finally there is the Book of the Revelation which could be called a prophetic book.

11

Progressive developments in the Bible

We have spoken of the unity of the Bible and of the uniform world view which it gives us throughout the ten or fifteen centuries of its composition. Another striking feature is the progressive development of revelation and the way in which it anticipates certain historical developments by centuries: it is as if revelation were joined to history, as it were 'wedded' to history, thus tracing a path for us to follow as we make our way through history. *"Quidquid recipitur, ad modum recipentis recipitur"* is a principle of philosophy. It simply means that the recipient receives as a recipient and not as a giver. In other words, if you have a ten-gallon barrel, you cannot put twenty gallons into it even if there are twenty gallons available; even if Einstein's theory of relativity is valid, you cannot explain it to a six-year-old boy, his mind is too 'small'; even if you have all the love in the world to give to someone, if that person is not open to your love, you cannot give it to him, he will not receive it. If the recipient is not open, if he is not ready, he cannot be filled. The same applies to divine revelation. God cannot reveal himself to the human race if human beings are not mature, ready and open to receive that revelation. God has to 'wait' and at the same time he has to educate us, help us to open ourselves until we become mature enough to receive that revelation. It is fascinating to read the Bible in this light; we can see that the writers of the Bible learn and grow as they write. And they learn and grow because they put into practice what is revealed to them.

12

Collective and individual responsibility

In this chapter and the following one, we shall give two examples of the progressive development of which we have been speaking, examples that could be multiplied.

The first example is the advance which humanity has made from a sense of collective responsibility — thinking of oneself as a member of a group — to individual responsibility — I am myself and responsible for my actions — which in its turn is tranformed into a new kind of collective responsibility but now with a full realization of one's own individuality and one's own responsibilities.

In so-called primitive tribes — and there lurks the primitive in each one of us — the individual has very little personal life as such, very little awareness of his or her individuality, he identifies with the tribe. If he becomes separated from it, he often dies. There is little personal identity because there is little conception of individual subsistence except at the animal level. This remains true in even the most highly developed ancient civilizations: we have only to think of what ostracism meant to the Greeks or exile to the Romans. In the medieval Church, excommunication played a similar role. (In passing, it should be noted that by excommunication the Church has *never* meant to prejudice one's chances of 'going to heaven'. Excommunication is *exclusively* concerned with the Church on earth. It means being excluded from the community of the faithful on earth, from the visible Church. As far as eternal life is concerned, the judgment rests with God, and the Church — contrary to popular belief — has never presumed to take this judgment upon herself.)

The idea of the individual emerged very slowly in the West. Already in the earliest times we find people, Socrates for example, and groups who are not only conscious of their own individuality but also teach others to be so. However, the vast majority of men had no conception of the individual person.

The idea began to spread in the early Middle Ages with the troubadours, and courtly literature marks an important advance. The knight loves his lady and idealizes her as a person. On the one hand we have the wife, who is part of the tribe, the collective, and on the other the *dame du coeur*, a personal relationship, which involves the giving of oneself and one's own loyalty to another individual.

At the end of the eighteenth century it can be said that for the first time in history, the concept of the individual person receives full recognition. The cry of *Liberté, Egalité, Fraternité* clearly implies an individual with his own rights and duties; man feels and believes himself to be his own master. This was a Western phenomenon and did not even include all the West; only after the Second World War, with the spread of education and Western culture, did this individual consciousness begin to extend to the whole world.

Freud is the best representative of the next stage. When his teaching began to be generally known, the individual started to look inside himself, to be occupied above all with himself; he separated himself from and was often hostile to his 'tribe', family, nation or group. This process had already started with the French Romantics, who suffered from *le mal du siècle*, but it became more acute and more widespread in the middle of the twentieth century. Then there came — and we are in the midst of it now — the need to return to community life; solitude has become unbearable. Everyone suffers from loneliness. But if people want community, they want their *own* kind of community, a community which will safeguard and protect their own personal demands. This is the dilemma which modern man is seeking to overcome.

e trace this historical progression in revela-
ll we have the Hebrews, a 'chosen people',
y collective in outlook. Individual sin has
ons on the whole community; the whole people is
ished for the sins of one man. And similarly the virtue
of one person reflects on the whole people of Israel. The
second stage, that of individual responsibility, is clearly
revealed to the prophet Ezekiel in 600 B.C. Let us read it:

> The word of the Lord came to me again: "What
> do you mean by repeating this proverb concerning the
> land of Israel, 'The fathers have eaten sour grapes,
> and the children's teeth are set on edge'? As I live,
> says the Lord God, this proveb shall no more be used
> by you in Israel. Behold, all souls are mine; the soul
> of the father as well as the soul of the son is mine:
> the soul that sins shall die. If a man is righteous and
> does what is lawful and right — if he does not eat
> upon the mountains or lift up his eyes to the idols of
> the house of Israel, does not defile his neighbour's
> wife or approach a woman in her time of impurity,
> does not oppress anyone, but restores to the debtor
> his pledge, commits no robbery, gives his bread to the
> hungry and covers the naked with a garment, does
> not lend at interest or take any increase, withholds his
> hand from iniquity, executes true justice between man
> and man, walks in my statutes, and is careful to
> observe my ordinances — he is righteous, he shall
> surely live, says the Lord God. If he begets a son
> who is a robber, a shedder of blood, who does none
> of these duties, but eats upon the mountains, defiles
> his neighbour's wife, oppresses the poor and needy,
> commits robbery, does not restore the pledge, lifts up
> his eyes to the idols, commits abomination, lends at
> interest, and takes increase; shall he then live? He
> shall not live. He has done all these abominable things;
> he shall surely die; his blood shall be upon himself.
> But if this man begets a son who sees all the sins which

his father has done, and fears, and does not do likewise, . . . he shall surely live. As for his father, because he practiced extortion, robbed his brother, and did what is not good among his people, behold, he shall die for his iniquity. Yet you say, 'Why should not the son suffer for the iniquity of the father?' When the son has done what is lawful and right, and has been careful to observe all my statutes, he shall surely live. The soul that sins shall die. The son shall not suffer for the iniquity of the father, nor the father suffer for the iniquity of the son; the righteousness of the righteous shall be upon himself, and the wickedness of the wicked shall be upon himself. But if a wicked man turns away from all his sins which he has committed and keeps all my statutes and does what is lawful and right, he shall surely live; he shall not die. None of the transgressions which he has committed shall be remembered against him; for the righteousness which he has done he shall live. Have I any pleasure in the death of the wicked, says the Lord God, and not rather that he should turn from his way and live? But when a righteous man turns away from his righteousness and commits iniquity and does the same abominable things that the wicked man does, shall he live? None of the righteous deeds which he has done shall be remembered; for the treachery of which he is guilty and the sin he has committed, he shall die. . . Yet the house of Israel says, 'The way of the Lord is not just'. O house of Israel, are my ways not just? Is it not your ways that are not just? Therefore I will judge you, O house of Israel, every one according to his ways, says the Lord God. Repent and turn from all your transgressions, lest iniquity be your ruin" (Ezekiel 18:1-30).

Now it is no longer the whole community but the individual who is made responsible for his own shortcomings. (The repetition is part of biblical style, but certainly the writer feels it necessary to repeat the concept again and again because the idea of individual responsibility is so new and so unacceptable.)

The third stage comes with Jesus. All his teaching points towards community life and that is how his disciples interpret it: "And all those who believed were together and had everything in common . . ." (Acts 2:44). But each person retains his or her own individuality and for Jesus each individual is infinitely precious simply as an individual; his relationships are always profoundly personal. How to respect the individual and at the same time seek the common good, was the problem facing the faithful in the Acts of the Apostles just as it was the problem of the members of the 'communes' in the United States in the sixties.

13

The three laws

There is a second example of progress, of growth, which can be clearly seen in the Bible. It both traces a path and can itself be seen as a line of progressive development. It is the passage from the law of the jungle to the law of Moses, fróm which point one can at least begin to understand the law of Christ.

For the person we incorrectly call 'primitive man' — in reality a part of man which runs through his entire history — the law of the jungle is what counts. This law means that the strongest gets the upper hand, the strongest wins. We are still primitive today and this law is often seen to be in force in individual, social and international relationships, in wartime for example.

During the Exodus from Egypt, Moses receives the law from God. The Hebrews are told not to follow the law of the jungle anymore but the law of 'an eye for an eye and a tooth for a tooth'. This law seems very harsh to us, but on reflection we can see that it represents a great step forward. Here a third person is introduced: a judge. The rights of the weak are respected; true justice comes into being. The Hebrews were not the first to introduce this sort of legislation; we can already find traces of it in the Babylonian Code of Hammurabi, five hundred years before Moses; but the Hebrews linked it with the justice of God and in consequence they drew up a whole series of laws which form the first real code of human rights. (Take for example the laws regarding slaves — who must be set free after a certain number of years — and also the laws regarding women.)

Jesus of Nazareth with his law, a law of love, shows us

the third stage of this development. In St Matthew's Gospel we read:

"You have heard that it was said, 'An eye for an eye and a tooth for a tooth'. But I say to you, Do not resist one who is evil. But if any one strikes you on the right cheek, turn to him the other also; and if any one would sue you and take your coat, let him have your cloak as well; and if any one forces you to go one mile, go with him two miles. Give to him who begs from you, and do not refuse him who would borrow from you. You have heard that it was said, 'You shall love your neighbour and hate your enemy'. But I say to you, Love your enemies and pray for those who persecute you, so that you may be sons of your Father who is in heaven; for he makes his sun rise on the evil and on the good, and sends rain on the just and on the unjust. For if you love those who love you, what reward have you? Do not even the tax collectors do the same? And if you salute only your brethren, what more are you doing than others? Do not even the Gentiles do the same? You, therefore, must be perfect, as your heavenly Father is perfect" (Matthew 5:38-48).

Perfection, then, consists in loving like this. Jesus demands the sort of behaviour which, from a human viewpoint, is absurd. People only behave like this when they fall in love or when they truly love one another. The experience of anyone who has loved is exactly this: we want to give everything to the person we love. We turn the other cheek; we give our coat as well as the shirt we were asked for; we forgive everything; we want to give our time and energy, our very life, without counting the cost. 'Justice', an eye for an eye and a tooth for a tooth, is no longer relevant or important. But it is only in personal relationships with family or loved ones that we can understand and accept this sort of behaviour. To extend this attitude to everyone seems utopian. The Gospel, however, suggests that this should be our normal way of behaving. While normally we are ruled by the law of the jungle moderated by a certain amount of 'justice', deep down we already know the conduct proposed to us by Christ, and in our better moments we long to put it into practice. One could describe Christianity as a power which serves to liberate people from the law of the jungle, leading them on to the law of love.

14

There is progress

If the people of the Old Testament, those of the Exodus and the Book of Judges, had been offered personal responsibility, they would hardly have known what to do with it; they would not have understood things like turning the other cheek. Human beings learn how to live progressively, over a period of time; revelation points the way but, as always, the signposts are fully understood only when one reaches the end of the road.

Thus Aristotle could not imagine a society without slaves; and although permanent slavery is rejected in the very first books of the Bible and Jesus strongly affirms the rights of the individual, it took one thousand eight hundred years of Christianity before Christians ensured that slavery was abolished (at least legally) throughout the world.

Despite the terrible state of the modern world, it is here that we can see progress, although we still have a very long way to go. Christians are only just beginning to understand (two thousand years after we were told to turn the other cheek) that pacifism is the only Christian response to war; also that the right to private property is not an absolute right (for example, see the encyclicals *Populorum Progressio* nos. 23-24 and *Laborem Exercens*, anticipated by St Ambrose of Milan in his *The Story of Naboth of Jezreel*); and it will probably take us another two thousand years to understand that money (that is, currency in the sense of material 'guarantee') is immoral.

As Aristotle — and probably St Paul, too — could not imagine a society without slaves, so we find the idea of a moneyless society completely utopian.

So in the Bible there is a progression, a call to growth; this progression, however, does not proceed in a straight line but spirally. And it is a twisted spiral. While man is still in the process of growth, while the recipient is taking shape, we can appeal to justice, wage wars, use money. (The first Christians, however, did not engage in lawsuits and often refused to do military service.)

But the closer we get to God, the more we learn to live by the law of love, the less we tend to have recourse to justice, to fight wars and to use money.

15

Definitions of God

It is well known that the Bible can be interpreted in many different ways, whether we take it as a whole or in its various parts. This is evident when we look at the history of a divided Christendom. From the earliest times, different groups of Christians have been at odds precisely because of differing interpretations of the Bible.

For a Catholic, the definitive interpretation is that of the magisterium of the Church and we shall deal with this in chapter 59. At this point it is enough to say that the Church's interpretation reflects a vision developed through the centuries and that very rarely has the Church given official interpretations of biblical passages.

The Bible, which is the revelation of God, speaks continually of God. In it we even find definitions of God, if one can call them that, which describe God in human terms. I find two of these definitions particularly striking: the first is very well known and comes from Exodus, one of the first books of the Bible, and the other is in the First Letter of John, written a few years after the death of Christ.

In the third chapter of Exodus, after God has appeared to Moses to tell him to lead the Hebrews out of Egypt to the Promised Land, there is the following dialogue: "Then Moses said to God, "If I come to the people of Israel and say to them, 'The God of your fathers has sent me to you', and they ask me, 'What is his name?' what shall I say to them?" God said to Moses, "I AM WHO I AM". And he said, "Say this to the people of Israel, 'I AM has sent me to you' " (Exodus 3 : 13-14).

First of all we should note that Moses, because of the

progression we have been talking about, would have understood that it was the god of his ancestors, Abraham, Isaac and Jacob, who was speaking to him; he would have understood that Yahweh was the name of his god. But he would not immediately have understood that this god was declaring himself to be the only God, the God of all mankind. We must remember here that *"quidquid recipitur, ad modum recipientis recipitur"*. The message is received only according to the capacity of the hearer. Centuries will pass before God's uniqueness is truly recognized; in fact, for a long time, this revelation of God's unity will be interpreted as if God were jealous and possessive. However, and this is what is so striking, the uniqueness, universality and timelessness of God is already present in the language of this text. And it is this understanding of God which, much later, will be so easily adapted to the system of classical metaphysics. This God calls himself 'I am', 'the one who is (present)'. (Does this mean that nothing else 'is'?)

The second definition which I find particularly striking is this: "Whoever does not love has not known God for *God is love*" (1 John 4:8). So God is this most mysterious thing which each one of us desires, which sustains and fulfills us more than anything else, which each of us wants to give and to receive, but which we can never really grasp or control or understand. What is more, it is said that even the knowledge of God is *necessarily* linked to this activity: loving.

These two things — being and loving — so central for our Western culture, are presented to us by the Bible as 'names' of God.

PART III
God's plan

In this third part, I would like to expound what recent theology calls 'the economy of salvation', or, more simply, God's plan for humanity. Here, too, I am giving only a rough outline without going into a lot of detail in an attempt to demonstrate each point as I go along. I am in fact presenting a viewpoint which, supposing it could be demonstrated, would be so by means of a theoretical structure such as that of Thomas Aquinas and even then only if it were set alongside a life lived from the same perspective.

We should remember that God is a mystery and that all we say about him and his activities cannot but be an incomplete affirmation both distorted and inadequate.

16

God loves

The Bible reveals Being as opposed to beings: there is an unbridgeable gap between them. God is the 'totally other', to quote Rudolph Otto.[1]

But it is also revealed that this God loves, he loves his creatures. He is a God whom we can contemplate with our minds; he also desires to enter into a personal relationship with every human being, with each one individually.

In the usual and also in the theological sense of the word 'create', God cannot create another God; if he creates, he can only create something 'less' than himself, that is, a creature. (A theology of the Trinity should be developed at this point; it is outlined in chapter 52.)

But if God, who loves, desires to have a loving relationship with his creature, the relationship must have these two characteristics: it must be free, and it must be a relationship between two people who are in some way equal. This is because freedom and equality are essential characteristics of love as we know it, and God, if he desires to love us and to be loved in return, has to love us on our terms, otherwise we would not be able to recognize it as love. (And that is another example of the way in which God has to adapt himself to human beings in order to be understood.)

So we must be able to choose God freely, with the corresponding possibility of being able to reject him.

1. Rudolph Otto, *The Idea of the Holy*, Penguin Books, 1959, p. 39f.

17

Man chooses

Man, we have said, must choose God. But can man choose? Certainly much in our lives is determined. We do not choose to be born, nor do we choose our heredity or social environment, nor our psychological make-up, etc. But knowing that we are able to make choices is an indispensable part of living, even if the question of free-will is one of the thorniest problems in Christianity and outside it.

If we choose trust, hope and love (which is God), we make room for God, we accept him and he can then unite us to himself. We have to choose God because we want God.

To choose or to reject. How can God give his creature the option of rejecting him? The answer to that dilemma is hell. The Church has always taught the existence of hell, but it has *never* given the names of anyone whom it believed had gone there; not even Judas Iscariot of whom a legend relates that he repented and so saved himself at the last moment. One is also reminded of the beautiful Roman proverb about suicide, "Between the bridge and the Tiber there is still the Grace of God", and of the epitaph of the Irish highwayman: "Betwixt the stirrup and the ground was mercy sought and mercy found".

Hell is the 'place' (mode of existence?) where God is *not*; where a person may choose to go if he rejects God.

The following comparison may help us to understand hell from a psychological point of view. We have all had the experience of the 'sulks'. Now we know that we get the sulks only with people we love, people who are important to us. We say to ourselves: "It's up to him to make the first move. Let him apologize . . ." and then, even when he does apologize, it is not enough. We want further proofs of submission and humiliation. This is where we come up against our own pride. It is pride which prevents us from 'making it up'.

Similarly, when we die, if we have allowed our hearts to become hardened (see chapter 63 on sin) then, just through pride, which is the only absolute sin, because we do not want to make our peace with God, we choose hell. God never sends anyone to hell; if hell exists, it is because God, out of love, respects our liberty.

18

Purgatory

To speak of hell as the guarantee of our liberty seems ridiculous. But if we look at it from Satan's point of view, perhaps we could say that hell, where the 'I' reigns supreme, is the only paradise; and paradise itself, a place where the 'I' is united in love with the Other and many others, would be hell for Satan (see chapter 36 on Satan).

A Catholic must say that hell exists, but can also say that perhaps there are no human beings there.

And since we are talking about liberty — and because it will help us to understand the preceding chapters — let us now speak of purgatory, trying to understand what it can mean for a Christian, and making use of our human experience here also.

When we are in love, we always want to look our best when we meet the loved one. When we are hoping to meet that person, we prepare ourselves physically and psychologically. We experience a most delightful anxiety. If we are dirty or untidy, we hurry off to wash or to tidy up, not out of fear but out of love. Now, when we die we 'see' God and we also see ourselves as we really are, that is, full of imperfections, defects and sins.

We hasten to wash, to clean and purify ourselves, to tidy ourselves up. This, in itself, is a painful process. As we wash ourselves we rub off some of our skin (this accounts for the tradition of physical penance). What is more, the loved one is waiting outside for us, we are anxious to join him; we each know how painful it is to keep a loved one waiting. When we die and we see ourselves as we are, we run to purgatory.

Purgatory is a gift of God because it enables our meeting with him to be free of feelings of guilt and shame. Thus going to purgatory is also a free choice on our part.[1]

1. U. Bonzi da Genova, *S. Caterina*: Edizione Critica dei Mano-scritti Cateriniani, Marietti 1962; J. Le Goff, *La Naissance du Purgatoire*, Gallimard 1981.

19

Life or death

Let us take up the thread of our argument again: we were saying that in order to have a loving relationship with us, God has to find a way to make us free and equal to him.

In order to resolve the problem of freedom, God invented hell. Which means that we choose God because we freely desire him, because we decide that life and love are values worth paying a high price for, the price being the hard work of living a human life.

God is Life, as the Old Testament tells us. He is what is. This also explains why suicide, if committed in full consciousness, is considered a sin. It is a choice against life and therefore against hope and against God (but see what is said about suicide in chapter 17).

Hell is death. It has always seemed extraordinary to me that in a world where hell was thought of as a place of fire and flames, Dante should have frozen Satan into a sea of ice — ice, rigidity, immobility, darkness, death.

So that is how God resolves the problem of liberty. He could not 'ask' us if we wanted to be born. But once we had been born, he made it possible for us to accept or reject life with him, that is, to agree or to refuse to open ourselves, to give, to share, to risk, in a word: to love.

But what of equality?

It is the Incarnation which resolves the problem of equality.

20

The bridge

Here we come to the heart of the specifically Christian argument, and to approach it from the angle of equality is to reduce it to an intolerable degree. God did not become man 'just' for that; he became man for much wider and more profound reasons.

He became man in order to re-create us, to bring us definitively out of nothingness; he became man to save us from sin and death. He became man for all the reasons we shall discuss when we speak of the sacraments and the Body of Christ. He became man because he is Love and only love can save us from nothingness and annihilation. These things are all interconnected; let us look at each of them in turn, beginning with the question of equality.

A successful love relationship is the total giving of one-self to another with the desire and hope, then fulfilled, that the other will for his part give himself wholly, so that the two 'may be one', and without the least hint of coercion (therein lies the freedom of love). It is, oddly enough, in the 'two made one', in a certain union, that each of the two people becomes fully person (see chapter 30 on love).

If there is no equality, love can never be mutually satisfied. Just think of the tremendous love some people have for their dogs: for human beings, such a relationship will always be incomplete, partial, because communication with a dog is limited, because there is no possibility of a total exchange, of total and reciprocal giving and receiving.

We have the same difficulty of inequality with God — even if, in this case, the positions are reversed. And one is always hearing people complaining about this inequality:

"How can we believe in something we can't see or feel, something so remote from us?"

God resolved this difficulty by becoming man. *"Et Verbum caro factum est et habitavit in nobis* — And the Word was made flesh and dwelt among us" (John 1:14).

God is the unthinkable, the unimaginable, the unintelligible, the unfathomable (the mystery both awesome and fascinating — in the strong sense of the word — as Rudolph Otto also tells us[1]). But Jesus of Nazareth can be touched, seen and heard: he has lived among us. It is not for nothing that the early Church constantly repeats: "He is like us". Here there can be knowledge, giving, receiving, exchange. Now we have something on our level which we can actually see, accept or reject, something to love or oppose or ignore. In this sense, Jesus is the 'way' to God, Jesus is the bridge, the 'pontifex'. In him everything is revealed. In him we see God in the measure in which, humanly speaking, one can 'see' God.

Certainly, God cannot be wholly understood at once even when he reveals himself in Jesus; so, after two thousand years, humanity continues to be fascinated by Jesus and has something to learn from Jesus. But now at least he is on the human level, he is 'flesh of our flesh'.

With the Incarnation, then, there is a tiny bit of equality between God and us. We have a bridge; a loving relationship between God and us is possible.

1. Rudolph Otto, *The Idea of the Holy*, ch. IV.

21

Love saves

And now we come to the crux of the argument — and it is not easy because it has so many ramifications which illustrate and complement each other. Like those drawings (Escher's for example) which, when looked at from different angles, represent different things, but the whole thing is a single, powerful drawing which one can never see as a whole and never quite grasp.

And this is the question: we have spoken of a loving relationship with God, but why ever does God want to have a loving relationship with us? It seems absurd even to suggest such a thing. Yet the Church teaches that this is the reason for creation: God created the world out of love, to manifest his 'glory', that is for himself, since, according to the Bible, he himself *is* love (see chapter 30 on egotistical love). *"Amor est diffusivum sui"*, says St Thomas Aquinas. Love seeks to diffuse itself. Love does not *need* to diffuse itself, but *desires* to do so (see chapter 29). Love desires to give itself, it does so out of generosity, just because it loves, not out of self-interest.

In the Christian vision of reality, creation is this diffusion of God's love. It is the loving God who desires to spread himself; so he creates in order to give and receive love.

In creation God reveals himself and expresses himself under the forms which we know in time and space. (These concepts could be linked with the philosophical and theological ideas of India; they, too, contain insights into this self-revelation and 'expansion' of God.)

Love is the mainspring of the whole of creation and the whole of Christianity. Love, this mysterious thing which we all know, which we all want, which each one of us wants to give and to receive, but which none of us understands.

Love creates and love saves. God creates and God Incarnate saves.

We know from experience that love creates and saves.

When we love and this love is returned, we feel fully alive, strong and whole. We are truly 'saved', we are 'something', we are what we should be, recognized, made real, rescued from nothingness. (See Hannah Green's very beautiful book *I Never Promised You a Rose Garden*,[1] with its realization that if people want to cure certain mental illnesses — here it is a bad case of schizophrenia — this can only be done by giving oneself to the sick person and thus 'saving' him. Love is a self-giving which heals and saves.) Love saves us, creates and re-creates us, brings us from nothingness to life.

On the other hand, when we lack love, we feel lost, desperate, crushed out of existence. Love is life and life is love and love is God. God, in giving himself to us, gives us life. But love is a gift which must be freely accepted, received and responded to. It is for this reason that God has to create first and then save. First of all God had to create a free person who could respond to his love; he had to make contact with someone in time and space, someone who would then be enabled to love, to be 'saved', to pass from the nothingness and death of time and space, to the life which is beyond both time and space.

Extending this vision still further, St Thomas Aquinas says that being, truth and goodness are interchangeable. This interchange is fascinating: love brings life and also brings goodness and truthfulness. The acceptance of life means the acceptance of goodness and love.

Christ is God, that is, love and life made visible. God creates, Christ re-creates and, with our free co-operation brings us life, goodness, truth. This process of re-creation by Christ is what is meant by 'salvation'.

Out of love, God desired (or had?) to create a transient world which passes away and dies, so that by dying it might be transformed into a real world, a permanent, immortal world, and this solely through the free and loving co-operation of his creatures. Creatures have to co-operate with the Saviour in order to save themselves from transience, nothingness and non-love.

1. Hannah Green, I Never Promised You a Rose Garden, Rinehart and Winston, 1964.

22

Christ the Way and the Life

We can look at the same thing from another point of view, the physical rather than the psychological. (However, I am chary of finding agreement or concordances between theology and science at any cost; see chapter 34.)

The world as we know it, at least according to one of the many scientific theories, is gradually grinding to a halt: this is called entropy. Everything is becoming colder and less mobile; the universe will end in total coldness and immobility — like Dante's Lucifer.

And here again we find God, first of all creating the transient and then, with our co-operation, re-creating, transforming and saving it. The Bible tells us that we came from nothing, and that we return to nothing is obvious when we see a dead person — cold and still. From nothing we return to nothing, if God does not save us. God wants to 'de-annihilate' us and the world, to finally create creation. And Christ is the way, he is the saviour.

By uniting ourselves to Christ in his mystical Body which is the Church, by means of its life-giving sacraments, we are saved from nothingness and death because we are joined to Life. So Christ is the Saviour because he saves us from our nothingness, and it is here (and not everywhere else, as people tend to think) that the idea of sin comes in.

Sin is an act of non-love which separates us from God by our own will, *never* his (see chapter 63). An act of non-love is a rejection, slight or serious, of that 'law of love' of which Christ spoke in the Sermon on the Mount (Matthew 5-6), and which we referred to in chapter 13. Sin is a rejection of God and also a rejection of truth and life as well as love. To be 'beyond' sin, to be beyond nothingness (and death), we must give willing adherence to the truth, to life and to love — in a word, to God and to Christ. It is in this sense (and let us not be scandalized by the words of Psalm 50) that we are all born 'in sin'. Christ, who is love, saves us from sin if we freely cling to him. If we remain in our sins, we certainly remain immobile, unloving, dead.

We already have life, that which our parents gave us, a life set in time and space. Even this life was originally given to us by God. (That Darwin was right and man evolved from other forms of life is certainly compatible with this affirmation.) But this life, in time and space, ends in death. Death is its necessary outcome. Each day we advance further towards death. In order to have a life which does not die, we need to be transformed and the thing which transforms us is love, human and divine.

When we are born, God gives us, so to speak, through our parents, the option of loving and living and being. If we accept love and live in love, if we accept God and live in him, we grow in love and our life is transformed into eternal life. If we reject love and life, we tend towards icy nothingness — hell.

Just because God cannot create another God and because love presupposes freedom — otherwise ours would be a world of puppets — God needs our co-operation in order to transform us into love, to deify us, to change us in some way into himself.

And because, in order to participate in such a transformation, we need to see and to feel, we need the material world, we need the Incarnation. It is through Christ that we are transformed into God. This is the deepest meaning of the word 'Saviour' as applied to Christ. He is not only the Way but also the Life (John 14:16). It is through Christ that God offers us his life and that we can most easily respond to his love (see chapter 70 on non-Christians).

Christ, then, is God's instrument in making us equal to him, and he is our Saviour, saving us from nothingness, sin and death. Christ is also our model. During his thirty-three years on earth, by living a life of love, by saving us, Christ shows us that love is humanly possible, that one can live lovingly. We can therefore take him as our model.

A model should always be in some way equal to those who are to copy it, and this is true of Christ. As we have seen, he is a bridge: he is both God and a human being.

If someone asks: "How should I act in this particular situation in order to act lovingly?", one can always reply with another question: "How would Christ act in these circumstances?" And if one is able to find the answer to the second question — not always an easy task (see chapter 45) — the answer will always be the right one. Christ is a model who has been incarnate in history, in the midst of human events, with all the political and social tensions we ourselves experience, in a world where various tendencies, forces and conflicts are at work. Here, too, Christ shows us the way, he is our model. Knowing Jesus, we have, so to speak, a live model of love. Not an explanation of love or an explanation of God, not a definition of God, but a living model of love: the Incarnation of God.

This presentation of Christianity in terms of love — a loving God who creates out of love and reveals himself out of love — is based both on biblical revelation, as we saw in the second part of this book, and on the post-biblical teachings of the Church. In order to demonstrate and fully develop such a vision, we would need volumes — by biblical scholars, theologians and mystics.

23

The Cross

And what about the cross?

The cross is so often placed at the centre of Christianity. This can make it appear to be a religion of pain, suffering and death instead of what it really is: a religion of joy and life. Certainly the cross is central to Christianity because it is through the cross that we come to the light, and "if the grain of wheat does not fall into the ground and die, it remains alone, but if it dies, it bears much fruit" (John 12:24). It should be stressed however that the cross is a means to an end, even if a necessary means. Instead there is a whole tradition which presents it almost as an end in itself. From the twelfth century onwards, in Western Europe at any rate, iconography concentrates much more on the suffering, crucified Christ than on the risen and victorious Christ. Sociologists, psychologists and historians could tell us why. What is certain, however, is that the major Christian feast is Easter Sunday, the feast of the Resurrection, and not Good Friday, and this has always been taught by the Church. Bearing this premise in mind, in order to understand the cross, we can follow various trains of thought.

1. The cross is the sign of man's condemnation. It is the symbol of what Yeats is referring to in his poem quoted in chapter 1: man must die, therefore all love is ephemeral, all hope illusory. But the Christian cross leads to the resurrection of Christ, and so *this* cross show that even if everything looks grim and all seems hopeless, from the Christian point of view, we need never lose hope altogether.

A danger arises here — and that is why Christianity has been accused of being the 'opium of the people':

we can find false consolation in this hope, running away from reality and hoping for 'pie in the sky'. But if we realize that the cross, that is, accepting and living rightly within one's own limitations, is the necessary condition for overcoming them and so rising again, then this danger vanishes; the cross then becomes the means of transformation and growth.

2. The cross also tells us that Christ, the model for us all, has had experience of difficult and painful situations at least comparable to our own sufferings.

3. On a deeper level, the cross is linked with considerations of autonomy (see chapter 29). The acceptance of the cross on Jesus' part is the highest and most concrete demonstration on the human level of the renunciation of one's own will in order to conform to that of the loved one — in this case the loved one is God. Christ accepts the will of the Father, emptying himself, says St Paul, to the point of death, the death on the cross (Philippians 2:8). And it is this total renunciation which totally liberates him and makes him most truly himself (see chapter 46).

4. Christ dies on the cross for the sake of 'justice', to show that the very fact that we are creatures destined to love, involves, if one is to live in the truth, the acceptance of our creaturehood and of our vocation of obedience to love, that is, obedience to God; it shows that submission is liberating while the refusal to love (which is sin), disobedience, is also a refusal of truth and justice.

There is certainly no need to think that the Father wants to 'avenge himself'; that the Son dies on the cross out of 'vengeance', so that the Father may be 'recompensed' for the sins committed by men. This death is the renunciation of self lived out to the full, a renunciation which is the expression of the willing desire on man's part to sacrifice all in the search for God, the search for love (for a consideration of the opposite choice, see chapter 62). On God's part, so to speak, the death of Christ, his Son, on the cross should show how even he is subject to his own law, that is, to his own nature. (God is what he is and he cannot act contrary to his own nature — here we are obviously speaking in human terms.) God 'submits' to justice, truth and love because God *is* justice, truth and love. Consequently, he cannot but require that we submit to truth, justice and love in order that we may be saved from untruth, injustice and sin, nothingness and death.

In this context, love is not possible without obedience. Christ submitted himself to the Father because submission is inherent in the logic of love and love is what God is (see chapter 29). God is a slave of love, so Christ is the slave of the Father in the Holy Spirit. But here 'slavery' has none of its usual negative connotations.

To renounce one's autonomy and one's independence in order to unite oneself to another does not mean to renounce either one's own personality or one's own will.

5. The cross is also the living answer to the great problem of the relationship between love and suffering. That all love involves suffering — even if it is often a 'sweet sorrow' — is a fact of universal experience (see the poem *The Rhinoceros* in chapter 3). But why does love involve suffering? Because all love, which tends to union, involves renunciation of self in favour of the loved one. And renunciation involves suffering.

Every life is full of examples of such renunciation; from the most ordinary, like the girl who gives up going to the cinema in order to join her boyfriend at a ball game which does not really interest her, to the person who lovingly spends many a sleepless night at the bedside of a loved one who is sick, to Christ who lays down his life for us all.

We deny ourselves, we suffer, but voluntarily, out of love, and therefore in a certain sense joyfully (this is certainly not masochism). It is in this sense that we must understand the saints who say that they love suffering; in this sense one can say that Christ on the cross, though certainly not happy, was joyful.

To experience this 'joy' of the cross, we must be near to sanctity. When we suffer, darkness and anguish prevail: 'we have lost our way'. Christ in the Garden of Olives is an example of this. Then comes the cross and the light.

To conclude: God is love, he created us to love and to be loved. In order to grow in love, we must accept the 'laws' of love — justice, truth.

This is painful for the individual — it crucifies us — but once we have accepted it, this cross brings us, in union with other men, to resurrection, to the presence of the God who is love.

24

Grace

Now let us try to see the meaning of grace, the Church and the sacraments.

The life of God is the true life, that which does not die. And as it is 'given', theologians call this life 'grace' (gift). Grace is God's life given to us. Now Christ, who is God (see chapter 52 on the Trinity), is grace in human form, Life incarnate in a human being. By choosing to share in his life, attaching ourselves to him, we will have true life.

There are many ways of interpreting this. One way is materialistically, as many of the Fathers of the Church did (see chapter 49). St Irenaeus of Lyon, for example, says: "For the mortal and corruptible to become immortal and incorruptible, it was necessary for the immortal and incorruptible to become mortal and corruptible". And St Maximus of Turin, wondering why Jesus submitted to baptism by John in the Jordan, as Jesus certainly had no need of baptism for the remission of sins, tells us that it was in order to sanctify water everywhere, so that every subsequent baptism would be able to draw grace from water now vitalized by Christ.

On the other hand we can interpret union with Christ, the gift of grace and the means of receiving grace, in a more spiritual way, where the emphasis is put on personal attitudes, intensity of feeling and the awareness of what is taking place.

The Church has always, though in varying degrees, tended to the materialistic interpretation. Over-spiritual interpretations have almost always led to heresies, that is, doctrines rejected by the Church (see chapter 66). To deny or underestimate our 'materiality' is always dangerous (see chapter 34). "*Qui veut faire l'ange fait la bête*", says Pascal.

For human beings who see and feel and perceive, Christ is the normal way of seeing God and entering into a loving relationship with God. As we have said, a loving relationship involves the gift of self to another person. In our loving relationship with God, we can now give ourselves to Christ, whom we can see and know. In return, Christ who is God gives himself, his grace and his Holy Spirit. The very words of the theological formula tell us this: Christ is grace 'made' man, the life of God 'made' man. And it is this life which is the true life.

With the coming of Christ all creation, and especially human beings, came into 'contact' with God, who is the fulness of life.

As we have seen, it is Christ who makes it possible for us to have a loving relationship with God on our own level, to develop our life for eternity. That is how he saves us from nothingness. As we shall see, it is he who is the only true Sacrament.

25

The Church

But Christ is no longer on earth. God knows that we human beings need constant contact, we need to touch: when we love someone, we want that person to be there all the time; and if the person is not there, we always want some kind of reassurance — a letter, a telephone call — not only for 'sentimental' reasons, but in order to continue our relationship which is, necessarily, developed through the 'material'.

Precisely for this reason, Christ has left two visible signs of himself: the Church and the sacraments, both vitalized by the Holy Spirit who is also God.

Something which has always struck me and of which I have never seen a theological exposition (except a little in the theology of the Eastern Church) is that Christian doctrine speaks freely of three bodies of Christ: the body of the historical Jesus now 'in heaven', the 'mystical' body which is the Church, and the body which is really present in the Blessed Sacrament.

Much has been written on these three bodies separately, but I have found very little on the relationship between the three. I find this an enormously interesting subject: however, at this point we can do no more than glance rapidly at the Church and the sacraments.

The Church is the Body of Christ which remains in our midst; the sacraments are one of the means whereby this Body acts visibly and efficaciously. It is here that we must see and feel Christ today. We should never separate these three things: Christ, the Church and the sacraments.

Unfortunately, historical events at various times and in various places have led many people to see the Church in a thoroughly negative and hostile light. Unable to see the Church as a whole, these people no longer see Christ or feel his presence. Instead of being a way, the Church here becomes an obstacle. I am not now referring to this sort of Church, or rather I am referring to it but not exclusively (see chapter 60).

It is true that the Church is an institution and that it is made up of visible buildings, but it is primarily a witness to Christ and an administrator of the sacraments.

The Church is the body of Christ made visible, and, in its saints and holy men and women, it acts with Christlike love; it bears witness, teaching and operating on the human level, administering grace in the sacraments on the super-natural level.

The Church consists not only of pope and bishops, priests and nuns; it is not just the buildings, but the whole 'people of God' as the Second Vatican Council insists on calling it. It is the totality of all the baptized in time and space, or, better still, in the ancient definition, it is the totality of all the members of the Church militant — here on earth — of the Church expectant — in purgatory — and the Church triumphant — in paradise. These three parts of the Church are inseparably linked together to form the Body of which Christ — risen and triumphant — is the Head.

26

The baptized

The Church is made up of all the baptized. Baptism is the sacrament which incorporates the individual into Christ and therefore into the Church, thereby saving him or her from nothingness, sin and death.

Christian doctrine has always held that baptism is necessary for all human beings in order to be saved and incorporated into Christ. However, it is not only the usual form, water baptism, which saves. As well as water baptism, in its various forms, there are two other kinds of baptism, by blood and by desire.

In the early Church and in recently Christianized countries (Uganda, for example, at the end of the last century and the beginning of this one), people died for their Christian faith before having received water baptism. Preparation for baptism was (and still is, for adults) quite lengthy, and some people were killed before having been baptized. It was taken for granted that by shedding their blood for Christ they were incorporated into Christ and so baptized. Many Christian martyrs in imperial Rome received the baptism of blood. The baptism of desire is received by those who seek God and truly desire him. And if anyone is put off by the word 'God', we can say that baptism of desire occurs if one desires and really practises goodness and truth as far as one is able, always striving for a deeper knowledge and a more perfect practice of these things. With the baptism of desire, then, everyone is in some sense a member of the Body of Christ. In this way we can overcome the horrible — and ridiculous — exclusivism for which so many preachers and catechists have been responsible.

Not that this is a new doctrine. Its roots may be found in the Acts of the Apostles (chapter 10) when the centurion Cornelius — much to St Peter's surprise — received the Holy Spirit *before* St Peter had baptized him with water. A more frequently quoted proponent of this teaching, though not the only one, is St Ambrose of Milan, who says in his funeral oration for the emperor Valentinian in 392 that although Valentinian had not been baptized, he had desired to be so and therefore had certainly received grace (M.L. 16, 1374). The Second Vatican Council confirms this development in the Constitution on the Church (*Lumen Gentium* II, 13-16), where it clearly states that all men are called by God and that all those who seek goodness and truth are in some sense incorporated into the Church — and so into Christ, thus finding salvation. (If this is so, we could well ask: "Why be a Christian if goodwill is enough for salvation? Why be baptized with water?" An answer may be found in chapter 70.)

27

The Sacraments are efficacious signs

So the Church is Christ and it is through the Church — in the Church — that we share in the life of God. This life is usually given to us through the sacraments.

We need to see and feel and touch. Matter is necessary for our understanding of things, for our growth and the expansion of our spirits — if we neither see nor touch nor communicate in some way with the loved one, love dies out eventually. The sacraments are visible and efficacious signs of the grace of God, so the catechetical formula tells us — signs of the life of God. They are visible for the reason we have just given. But at the same time they are also symbolic (see chapter 57), and they are efficacious as well. The red traffic light would be efficacious if it not only showed red but also activated the brakes of the car. The sacraments are efficacious: they effect what they signify. Baptism really washes and makes fruitful; confirmation gives strength; the Eucharist nourishes and invigorates: it *truly* gives Life.

We can only accept the efficacy of the sacraments if we accept the divinity of Christ. There are no 'proofs' of their efficacy. The proof lies in living them; it is by living them that we experience their efficacy. (Here, too, it is obvious that the unbeliever can put the whole thing down to mere psychological experience.) If Christ is just a man, the sacraments are at the most mere symbols, reminders of him or of actions performed by him. If, on the other hand, Christ is still the living God, if Christ is risen, then the sacraments are efficacious. They are the actions of Christ, transcending time and space and yet coming to us again and again *in* time and space.

As the divinity of Christ has no meaning for someone who does not believe in the existence of God, so the efficacy of the sacraments can have no meaning if one does not believe in the divinity of Christ. But if one does believe in it, everything unfolds with surprising harmony, and matches up with our experience of love. This is one of the coherent aspects of Christianity which struck me so forcibly before my baptism.

After the death and resurrection of Christ, it is the Eucharist in the Church which is the central sign — both visible and efficacious — of God's presence on earth. And it is the Eucharist which is the essential nourishment and the central devotion of the whole Church. It is by means of the sacraments, especially the Eucharist, that we have our 'material' link with God (see chapter 34).

The whole thing can also be looked at in this way: the only true sacrament is Jesus of Nazareth. He is the visible, tangible and audible sign of the life of God — he and only he. And he is the visible and efficacious sign of the life of God because he is the incarnation of God. Jesus is the only sacrament, and the sacraments as we call them are none other than Christ himself, acting through such agents as water, bread, wine, oil and the various members of his Church who preach and administer the sacraments: bishops, priests and laity, according to the needs of the whole Church and those of its individual members.

When Christ acts he is efficacious. The sacraments give us God's life; they draw us out of nothingness. But even the sacraments are always acts of love and so subject to the laws of love, among which is the freedom of any act of love. However efficacious the sacraments may be, they don't 'take', their efficacy does not 'work', if the person who receives them is not truly open to them. If someone confesses with no real sorrow, without serious intention of amendment, it is certain that the absolution will be worthless, or rather it will be a sacrilege. In a baby baptized at birth, baptism in certain respects is immediately efficacious (for example, it 'washes'); in other respects it is efficacious only when the child starts to perform acts of the will. But grace is there from the start, available in order to be used when possible (see chapters 56 and 57).

To sum up: Jesus of Nazareth, the only true sacrament, the efficacious source of true life, both visible and tangible, is no longer on earth. Knowing our need of the visible and tangible, he has remained among us in two forms: the Church and the sacraments. The Church and the sacraments are the visible extension of the Body of Christ on earth, vitalized by the Spirit; they are our source of eternal life.

28

Death is defeated

To conclude this third section: God's plan for humanity is to divinize it, and this is probably his plan for all creation (see Romans 8: 19-26). God creates every human and non-human being out of nothing. We must co-operate with God, use the material of which we are made, use the things around us, from rocks to fellow human beings; by means of love and with the help of God's grace, we have to make them and make ourselves into something divine. "You shall love God above all things and your neighbour as yourself"; this is the meaning of all the law and the prophets. Christ is the way. The good news — gospel means 'good news' — is this: with God we can, if we want, go beyond the limitations of human life and natural phenomena to get to what lies behind them, the numinous: we can break through the horrible barrier of death and come to eternal life. Christ is the way and love is the means to get there.

PART IV

Further thoughts

This fourth part is made up of small chapters which are a commentary on what has gone before and also starting points for further reflection. They are only quick notes. I am not setting out to give an exhaustive treatment of what I say but merely to add a few strands to the material being woven, a few extra pieces to the puzzle, a few more tiles to the incomplete mosaic.

Each person has to weave his own garment, complete her own puzzle or mosaic. The frame of the picture and the hem of the garment must be left undefined, open to adjustment because our perception and understanding of theological, philosophical, artistic and human truth, change and broaden daily; definite limits tend to deafen and blind one to the truth, even though such limits may reassure us.

On the other hand, to leave things too open and too vague, prevents us from grasping and understanding truth, so we also need to be precise, to circumscribe, to reach conclusions, to make definite statements.

We cannot understand and construct a system of thought without starting with a particular strand or a particular framework, but we must always have the humility to see that neither strand nor framework is definitive. The following outlines are intended to help each reader to make further clarifications, definitions and decisions of his own.

29

Autonomy and pride

God created us in his own image and likeness. So we should not be surprised that we should aspire to be like God, even to *be* God: that is, to think and do everything that we want to do. We naturally want not only to be free but also to be entirely independent and autonomous.

This is the terrible dilemma in which everyone is trapped, and, according to tradition, this applies to every rational creature, including the angels.

The truth is that every person and every creature derives its existence, not from itself but from another: from its parents in the first instance and originally from God. We are not entirely autonomous; our origin and source are not in ourselves. In all honesty we cannot deny this, so we have to recognize that we are creatures before being creators. To begin with, we are dependent, not autonomous. To persist in affirming the opposite is pride, the root sin.

If we insist on our autonomy and affirm it, we are giving assent to a lie because our autonomy is not in fact real. In Arabic Satan is the Lord of Lies — Baal Zebub.

To affirm our autonomy is to impoverish ourselves because, being outside the truth, we cannot live in love — love is truth; goodness and truth are interchangeable.

God's solution — the loving one — is simple: one acquires one's own autonomy by giving oneself trustfully to love. This is the basis of the act of faith.

It is reasonable to trust God and it fits in with our psychology: if God is the way we have described him, he knows us better than we know ourselves and loves us more than we love ourselves. So it shows wisdom on our part if we have complete confidence in him. He desires our fulfilment, our full development, that is, our freedom.

Let us also remember that the Christian God is not an omnipotent God in the absolute sense (I am using human terminology) but is himself subject to the 'laws' of his own being, which are the laws of love. So he can give us our freedom only in the measure that we give him our trust; in the measure that we accept the truth, accept him and unite ourselves to his will — which is both absolute goodness and good for us in particular.

Our free submission in a relationship of love is the vindication and affirmation of our desire for autonomy. Where autonomy, independence and individualism impoverish, sterilize and deaden us, the gift of self, dependence and union liberate, nourish and invigorate us.

Another word for this submission is obedience.

30

There is no such thing as pure love, love is always selfish

It is said that love is always selfish. In one sense, that is absolutely true. And it is true in the sense that selfishness means seeking to win something for oneself. The person who loves always wins. However, when one loves, one is seeking not primarily one's own advantage but love; one is continually hoping to 'win' the other person's love. Love, as we said, is the encounter and union between two people. The greater the love, the greater the unity and the closer the union. They want the same things for each other; they share the same tastes, the same thoughts and the same world view, not by relinquishing their own personality but, on the contrary, by receiving and gaining fulness, even super-abundance, from each other. I am thinking of those old married couples who after years and years of living and loving together even end up looking like each other; and, what is even more beautiful, they often die within a few days or a few hours of each other. They have lived out their love and brought it to perfection.

God's love is like this. When he loves, God 'glorifies' (manifests) himself in this way. The more he gives us, the more we reflect his love and the more we glorify him. On the other hand, the more we give ourselves to him, the more fulfilled and glorious we ourselves become.

In the perfect relationship — the Trinity — the Persons both give *and* receive love perfectly; they are one and yet three (see chapter 52).

So selfishness here does not mean grabbing, possessing, hoarding, keeping for oneself. Rather, this kind of selfishness realizes that by fulfilling the 'self' of the loved one, one is fulfilled oneself. In this sense, all love is selfish, especially the love of God; the catechism tells us that God created everything for his *own* glory and St Paul in the Letter to the Colossians (1:15-20) and St John in his Gospel (1:1-13) develop and elucidate this affirmation.

31

Eternal life

People often ask me — frequently the family when someone dies — "What is eternal life like? Where do people go? Can dead people see us?"

I always answer by giving this example, which I originally heard from an Orthodox priest in Paris. Let us imagine that the person who asks is called Joanne and is exactly twenty-eight years old. I tell Joanne: "Twenty-eight years and three months ago, you were in total darkness, immersed in fluid. You were fed through the umbilical cord. All you could hear were muffled sounds, and you were so closely joined to someone else that you could truly be said to be a part of that person. Well, then, if someone had been able to get in touch with you and say: 'Joanne, in a few months, you will be in the light, you will eat through your mouth, you will breathe air and in a few years you will be able to drive a car, eat chocolate and go to the cinema', do you think you would have been able to understand any of that?"

No. And the reason is that life in the outside world is completely incomprehensible to an unborn child (*Quidquid recipitur . . .*).

The same applies to eternal life. We know that we shall lose our body as we know it, as we have already lost the amniotic sac, the amniotic fluid and even the umbilical cord. And yet, here we are. What will the next life be like? I do not know. He whom I believe to be the only person to have risen from the dead has perhaps given me a few clues. To start with, I believe in the resurrection of the body (and not only of the 'soul') — and, after death, he ate fish, could be seen and heard (see the marvellous passage in Luke 24:13-33 and also the doubting of Thomas in John 20:24-29); yet he passed through closed doors and disappeared at will. It seems as if, in the end, we shall attain complete mastery of our bodies and their functions, and will be able to do what we want with them.

I don't know at all what eternal life will be like, I only know that we have already made a similar passage at our birth and that 'eternal life', which is also material but where we can control matter as we know it, fits in with all we have said so far.

32

When will the dead rise again?

The dead will rise again 'at the end of the world', 'at the end of time'. Yet Mary has already been 'assumed' into heaven and the Church tells us that the saints are already able to intercede for us. Why are they 'already' able to do this if they are still lying in their graves or in the shrines in churches, awaiting the resurrection?

We can solve this problem if we remember how we are immersed in time, slaves of time. We are incapable of thinking 'outside' time. But after death we are *outside* time and space; time does not 'pass' for God, God is always 'young' (religious art has often represented the Trinity as three young men). The resurrection of the dead lies ahead of us, but for the dead this is probably not so. They are 'beyond' time and space. So it is meaningless to ask 'when' the resurrection of the individual will take place.

33

Extra-terrestrial creatures

People often ask me if the belief in the existence of other inhabited worlds is compatible with Christian theology. The answer is definitely yes. What is more, one could very well argue that the Church has always believed and taught that there are extra-terrestrial beings. When the Bible tells us of angels, when St Paul and the liturgy speak of cherubim and seraphim, thrones and dominations, they are talking about intelligent creatures of a different species from us men (see St Thomas' treatise on angels) which in modern parlance could very well be called Martians or other types of extra-terrestrial creatures.

"Quidquid recipitur, ad modum recipientis recipitur": it is clear that the biblical writer and liturgist of the early centuries would have given wings to their Martians rather than helmets and missiles.

34

Matter and spirit

Many people, at least in the West, divide reality into matter and spirit. This division is one of the ways in which we interpret our perceptions of reality. If the world were really all 'spiritual' (that is, if what we perceive as two distinct things were in reality just one thing), I do not believe it would make any difference to the truth or untruth of Christianity. (If it were all 'material', of course Christianity would be nonsense.) In other words, the distinction between matter and spirit seems to me to be irrelevant to the essence of Christianity.

There are two important cultural traditions which we can follow here: the philosophical, taken in the broadest sense, and the scientific.

In the Hebrew world view of the Old Testament, although the distinction between the material and the spiritual certainly exists (God is *not* material), the distinction is not as clear as in Greek thought; and the Hebrews would have disagreed — had they known of it — with the prevalent Indian view which utterly denies the objective reality of the material world.

The repeated affirmations at the beginning of the Book of Genesis (1 : 12-31) that everything that God created is 'good', serve not only as a safeguard against a Manichean type of dualism but also serve to enhance the value of the material world.

In the modern world, philosophy does not usually make a distinction between the material and the spiritual worlds. Moreover, modern science has shown us that the things we see are not what they appear to be — for example, they are all reducible to electrons and protons grouped in various ways, they are governed by magnetic fields, etc. In fact, we do not know what matter really is. What we see is reality as organized by our senses of perception. When we apply these scientific discoveries to the distinction between matter and spirit, we find that the distinction itself is invalidated, or at least blurred.

But I do not wish to fall at this point into a trap where theologians have often fallen: scientific 'concordism'. That is, a scientific discovery is made and theologians immediately try to appropriate it and make it agree with theology. So in the last century when the atom was discovered, people tried to say that it was the 'atoms' of the bread which — after the consecration — were transformed into the 'atoms' of the Body of Christ! This is not only absurd — you *cannot* align theology and science like that — but it is also dangerous because when the scientific theory is discarded or else expanded in some way, it no longer fits.

However, bearing in mind this danger, I believe that one can say that everything we call 'spiritual' should be approached with caution. What I mean is that the material may be an expression of the spiritual; matter and spirit, then, are not necessarily two separate things, different from each other. Can one say that the eye is 'matter' and the look 'spirit'? Or consider the very beautiful Buddhist example which relates to this problem: what exactly passes from the seal to the wax? Yet the seal remains imprinted on the wax.

So God manifests himself in nature, in human beings, but *in* time and space, that is, in a way that is transitory, incomplete, impermanent — corruptible and mortal as St Irenaeus of Lyon would say. Now the central tenet of Christianity is, as we have seen, that God takes hold of the transitory and, co-operating with the Spirit which is in us (and in things? see Romans 8:19-22), seeks to work with the freedom which he has given us, in order to transform the transitory into the permanent, in what we call a love-relationship.

The division of reality (the world) into matter and spirit does not reflect what the word (reality) is, but merely how we perceive the world. It is a distinction, a division, which *we* make.

In conclusion: the material and the spiritual worlds are not two worlds but only one; they are two constantly inter-penetrating aspects of reality.

And, to go a step further — which will involve much further clarification — the natural and supernatural worlds are but one world. For a Christian at least, after the coming of Christ, the natural world is as it were impregnated with the supernatural. Our way of looking at things tends to make us divide things into matter and spirit (natural and supernatural). But as I said at the beginning of Part IV, if we have to construct outlines, divisions and limits — in this case to divide into two — in order to understand the world, we should also remember that these divisions, limits, frames, are not definitive but merely structures to aid comprehension and to serve as a basis for future growth and expansion of the understanding.

35

Is there such a thing as objective truth?

From all that I have said so far it will be obvious that my answer to that question is yes.

Modern man assesses truth by asking himself if a thing is demonstrable and/or verifiable: there are five people in this room and he counts them: one, two, three, four, five. H_2O = water: he analyzes it and demonstrates that this is so. In a right-angled triangle the square of the hypotenuse is equal to the sum of the squares on the other two sides, and so on.

For modern man, roughly speaking from Descartes onwards, the criterion of truth is so-called 'scientific' demonstrability. And for the man in the street this is still the criterion today. It is only at the highest levels of scientific thought and research that the equation: truth = demonstrability, is known to be false.

It was in the 1920's and 1930's that scientific certainty first began to be questioned. Einstein's theory of relativity, non-Euclidian systems of geometry, Heisenberg's principle of indetermination, Godel's theorem, all shed doubt on the scientific 'certainties' which seemed to have been established. As a result, many began to deny the existence of objective reality, despising the sciences and philosophies which postulated such truths, and maintaining that if there is such a thing as objective truth, it is unknowable and therefore does not concern us.

On the other hand, there was talk of certain patterns which apply to particular situations and which are 'truth' for that particular thing and in that particular situation.

These patterns, along with recent efforts to 'unify' reality into a single pattern, as well as other similar ventures, are extremely interesting as they approach our present problem from a completely different angle; but at the moment they are of interest mainly to mathematicians and philosophers. People on the whole are sceptical about any sort of 'truth' presented to them.

For my part I maintain that truth is one — truth is God. God is love, God is being. Truth is love, truth is being. *Bonum, unum, ens, verum inter se convertuntur* — Goodness, oneness, being and truth are interchangeable — as we have seen.

And the revelation of God is also truth. "I am the Way, the *Truth* and the Life!" (John 14:6). So truth is love, truth is Christ. Truth is not something we acquire only by knowledge and study (it is certainly *also* acquired by knowledge and study) but by living and loving to the full. We grow in truth in the measure that we grow in love, that we grow in goodness, that we grow in knowledge, that we grow in life. So no one can say I 'know' the truth, I 'have' the truth; one can only live the truth by living lovingly. But truth exists and it is one truth, not many truths, although human beings, being unable to grasp all of the truth (because they cannot 'understand' God), only see different facets of it and from different points of view. But if they are really true, these different facets and points of view can be reconciled among themselves.

In strictly Christian terms, we could say that since Christ is the truth and the Church is the Body of Christ, there is a precise sense in which the Church contains the truth and is the depository of the truth. But not because the visible Church is always 'true' (see chapter 60) and even less because 'churchmen' possess the truth or are necessarily the measure of the truth.

36

The fall of Satan

The myth of the fall of Satan is a great help towards our understanding of original sin, pride and autonomy (see chapter 29). We could also study this by means of the great Fausts of literature as portrayed by Marlowe, Goethe, Valery, Mann, etc., where Faust desires power, not so much to dominate others (pride can also take the form of false humility) but in order to be self-determining; he wants to be his own master he wants to be autonomous.

Tradition tells us that Satan's cry is *"non serviam"*, I will not serve. For someone who does not love, dependence means service in the sense of servitude (see chapter 67).

Thi is how an old French Dominican described to me the sin of Satan, Lucifer, the most beautiful of all the angels: he looked at himself in the mirror and did not want to see anything else, he said *"Moi"*, Me, and then he fell.

37

Qohelet or Ecclesiastes

Qohelet (or Ecclesiastes, as it is called in many bibles) is one of the wisdom books (see chapter 9). Its subject is the vanity of things and of the world: "Vanity of vanities, says Ecclesiastes, vanity of vanities! All is vanity" (1:2). It is one of my favourite Old Testament books (perhaps my favourite), and I am not alone in this: dozens of authors quote or use passages from it.

Sometimes people are surprised to find this book in the Bible at all, and this is because the writer seems to be without hope. All is vanity: "Better to be a live dog than a dead king". It could be a Buddhist book, as it could lead one to the thoughts of renunciation and despair experienced by the Buddha (see chapter 2) when he encountered old age, illness and death.

And it really is like that; reading it makes one feel like that. (And for that reason it has a very modern ring.)

I think a Christian can read the book in the following way.

The history of Israel, as we have seen, is a progressive history (see chapter 4). Its point of departure — and we did not look at this — is Abraham's vocation (Genesis 12), the impulse which drives him on and the promise made to his descendants: "I will give this land to your descendants", a land which is later described as "a land flowing with milk and honey" (Exodus 13:5). Qohelet, writing between 250 and 200 B.C., fifteen hundred years after Abraham, saw the fulfilment of those promises. They have the Promised Land, they have the milk, they have the honey; yet all this is nothing, it is all vanity. Qohelet who, like nearly all the Old Testament writers, has no clear belief in eternal life, knows, like Yeats (see chapter 1), that man loves things which will vanish.

Qohelet seems to me to be uttering a cry, or rather a scream, howling for a way out of this closed box which is the world and this closed circle which is life. Behind him, certainly, stretch fifteen hundred years of promises fulfilled. But he can see nothing beyond, no open door anywhere. How does one transcend this world? How does one escape from this absurdity?

For a Christian the answer is obvious; it is that someone should come from 'beyond' and come *into* this world and open up the closed circle: the answer is the Incarnation. But Qohelet cannot even imagine it.

Another interesting thing about this book, which relates it to Buddhism and to all the Oriental religions, is its cyclical vision of time: everything repeats itself: "there is nothing new under the sun".

Orientals see time, or history, as a wheel from which one never escapes. It is the Hebrews — Abraham — who are the *first* (was this revelation or a discovery?) to see time as a straight line and therefore progressive; so they were the first to give meaning to history.[1]

Now Qohelet, in accordance with his near-despair, turns towards the past, and of all the biblical books his is the only one which has an almost cyclical vision of time. Again it is Christ who transforms history from a circle to a straight line, but with a line which passes through the cross — which is not vanity — and returns full circle whence it came — to the Father.

1. See Mircea Eliade, *The Myth of the Eternal Return*, Pantheon Books, 1954.

38

Job

Job, like Qohelet, is one of the wisdom books of the Old Testament (see chapter 9). It is a story, probably of semitic origin, which has been taken up and elaborated by the Hebrew writer. Job is not a Hebrew but he is 'just'. We see from this that the ancient editors of the Bible, even then, believed that God is interested in all men — he desires that all should be saved as St Paul will say (1 Timothy 2:4) — and, in an absolute sense, he does not favour the children of the Chosen People above all others. But important though this is, it is not the central teaching or the main interest of this book. It deals above all with the problem of evil and suffering.

Job is a good, honest pagan who has never offended the Lord. He is very wealthy: he has lands, livestock, sons, nephews, everything which means wealth in the East. He is also a man who adores and fears God (see chapter 67). The tempter — Satan, who is still referred to here as a son of God — maintains that since Job has everything, it is easy enough for him to adore God; if he were to lose everything, he would no longer do so. Satan gets permission to destroy first Job's wealth, then his sons, and finally to inflict terrible illnesses on him, as long as he does not take his life.

Satan's plan doesn't work. Job, sitting on a dunghill, with all his goods destroyed, all his children dead and his body racked with leprosy (or cancer), still does not offend God. He repeats these words: "God has given, God has taken away, blessed be the name of the Lord" (which makes his wife say he is stupid).

Then comes the real theme of the book: forty chapters of argument by various people who seek Job out to discuss the reason for all his misfortunes. Why does Job, a 'just' man, suffer? It is taken for granted that evil *cannot* come from God if there is no guilt, so Job's interlocutors try to show that he has sinned in some way in order to have deserved all these ills. Their arguments are frequently shallow, but at times the problem is approached with a great deal of subtlety. However, the problem is *not* resolved. Job protests and defends himself: "I have never offended God". At one point he even starts to argue with God and God answers by speaking of his own power and above all of man's inability to 'understand' God. So God does *not* give an answer, the Bible only poses the problem, with great clarity however. God remains silent. A wise old Carthusian once told me that the Book of Job teaches us that the silence of God, for those who open themselves to him, is more consoling than any words we can speak.

39

Evil

At the end of the preface to this book I said that if Catholicism is not true, it is certainly coherent, and that even now I don't know if it is true.

Why don't I know? For two reasons: the first, which is semantic and ordinary enough — though it is based on the very complicated and difficult problem of epistemology inconclusively treated by Berkeley, Locke, Hume, Kant and others — is this: what is knowledge and what, consequently, is truth? I have given my answer in chapter 35.

The second reason — and this is the great stumbling-block for so many — is the problem of evil.

In the Bible there are two writers who explicitly pose this problem — Job and Ecclesiastes (see chapters 37 and 38) — and neither of them resolves it.

Evil has been the subject of endless discussions down the centuries, the Christian view being expressed at length by Augustine (especially in his anti-Manichean writings) and Thomas Aquinas (for example, 'De Malo' in Questiones disputatae). They both shed real light on the subject but certainly do not resolve the problem in all its endless ramifications.

The 'intelectual' answers to the problem are not satisfying, although St Thomas' answer is undoubtedly brilliant.

Jung tried to write an answer to Job but his answer is not one of his best works. C. S. Lewis' The Problem of Pain[1] treats the matter more exhaustively, but not much more so.

Humanity is tormented by the problem of evil and the related problem of pain. There are natural disasters like the earthquakes which claim thousands of victims every year, causing death, injury and homelessness. Couldn't God have made the earth 'stable'? And think of all the thousands of different diseases. All, or nearly all, of us have seen the long and painful sufferings of someone dying of cancer. Add to that all the psychological and moral sufferings and it is useless to prolong the list.

Dostoyevsky, and later Camus, put the problem like this: the cry of one suffering innocent child proves the non-existence of God.[2]

Is there any answer? I cannot find one which is total and satisfying.

I can only offer — as I do in this whole book — what I myself 'answered' before I 'accepted' God.

First of all, let us distinguish between evil and suffering.

As far as Dostoyevsky's and Camus' problem is concerned, there is evil where there is suffering: an earthquake in the middle of the Sahara, however violent and widepread, would not be evil in itself because it would have no victims.

Theology, however, would say that evil occurs every time there is sin (see chapter 63). When the pain caused by sin is not evident, theology tells us that the suffering — in this case, redemptive — has been borne by Christ on the cross (see chapter 23) and by his Body which is the Communion of Saints (see chapter 55).

Evil generates suffering 'genetically' and/or in a 'socio-cultural' way.

1.   There are the sins of individuals which, since the time of Adam, have been mounting up, often resulting in an accumulation of evil. For example, a dissolute man becomes an alcoholic and will perhaps have a son whose health is impaired, which will make the life of the son and those around him much more painful and difficult. In this sense, the biblical saying that the sins of the fathers will fall on the children is quite true. And they spread like an oil stain because they affect everyone around.

2.   We must add to this all the social and ecological evils: lazy and corrupt politicians and bureaucrats, employers who exploit their workers, doctors and teachers

who have a shabby or inhuman approach to their profession, the general corruption caused by those who are habitually mean: here evil has repercussions on the whole of society and is added to the sins of individual people. Evil is something which spreads. Now God could intervene in two ways: either by 'punishing' every evildoer on each occasion, and then very few of us would go unpunished, and even if we were allowed to live, we would walk in constant fear (see the myths of the universal flood); or he would have to take away our freedom in order to prevent us from doing evil, making puppets of us all. In fact the greater part of our ills is directly or indirectly caused by ourselves — the result of our abusing our freedom.

3. But there *is* something else: the sufferings caused by earthquakes, the sufferings of the innocent and the fundamental question: "Why does the good man suffer?"

I can find no answer to the evil and the consequent suffering which is not attributable to human beings. Only an image someone suggested to me years ago seems to contain a grain of truth and throws some light on the subject, but even this does not resolve the problem: "God created the universe in perfect equilibrium. The whole thing was suspended, like a huge egg, by springs attached to the inside of the shell. When Lucifer rebelled (or when Adam sinned), one of the springs gave way and everything was left poised, in disorder, suspended in the most precarious way."

So this means that there is disorder in the universe, in creation, and intelligent beings — Christ, the angels, men and women — have to re-establish order by means of love.[3]

When it comes to the suffering of good men, I find it easier to give an answer. Christ can enlighten us here, as can our own experience of the relationship between love and suffering.

Suffering — *not* evil, but the suffering which is the result of evil — if it is accepted, is redemptive and constructive.

On the one hand, suffering detaches us from things and makes us freer (it liberates us from slavery); and on the other hand it helps us to see things more clearly and so to act with greater assurance and effectiveness. This applies equally to an ordinary punishment which is not entirely justified but which we accept, and to the deepest of sorrows. That suffering can be redemptive is probably the main lesson we have to learn from Christ's death on the cross, though it is not the main theological reason for his death (see chapter 23, nos. 3 and 4).

A priest probably has more opportunity than others to see instances of this truth. I have in mind the example of two persons who grew in wisdom and deepened their lives in a way one would never have expected by accepting the life and death at two years of age, of a much desired only son who was born a mongol.

The suffering of a good man also has pedagogic value (is that not the case with Job?), for it can be seen as a passage towards the light by way of the cross which is perhaps the only way of salvation if our freedom is to be preserved (see chapter 23, no. 3). This does not explain evil, nor does it justify it. It merely tells us that evil is not necessarily destructive and that it can even be constructive.

There remains one sort of evil, one sort of suffering, which cannot possibly be called constructive — or at least so it seems to us — the suffering of a cancer patient, for example, who comes to the point of cursing God.

At this point there comes to my mind the proverb: "Better to have loved and lost than never to have loved at all".

We must remember that we cannot think of God except in human terms, in the categories of human psychology. In *these* terms, I think that from God's point of view, when all is said and done, the whole creation and all the good which comes from it, the love and beauty and virtue which it brings forth — all this is worth the residue of suffering and pain, and this 'residue' includes the suffering of Christ, his Son.

But who can say what suffering looks like from outside time and space?

I cannot go any further. Here I have to make a real act of faith. I have one theological problem: seeing there is so much suffering in the world and knowing that God could have chosen *not* to create it, why did he choose to create it?

Having chosen to create the world, he had to give us freedom if we were to love, whence the possibility, indeed the probability, of evil and sin and suffering. (Let us remember that in the biblical view, Lucifer is the cause of evil and suffering in the world and perhaps other parts of the creation are too, for evil is not a problem confined to human beings; see chapter 36.)

It seems that God, being love, preferred to have "loved and lost a little, than never to have loved at all".

1. C. S. Lewis, *The Problem of Pain*, Macmillan, 1943.
2. For example, Albert Camus, *The Plague*, Hamish Hamilton, 1948.
3. See Charles Williams *War in Heaven*, Faber and Faber, 1947.

40

The obscurity of faith

Theologians call the problem of the act of faith the 'crux theologorum', their cross. This is because, according to classical theology, there are three parts to an act of faith: reason, will and grace. When a person says "I believe" what part does each of these three elements play in the act of faith?

Some people know all about theology with their minds, they even find revelation reasonable, but they do not have faith, they cannot say "I believe". Many others would like to believe; they pray and do their utmost to believe but they do not believe.

Then there are those — like me for example — for whom believing is so obvious, so simple, that they have no real problems (there *are* problems, big ones, but they are *within* one's belief).

In fact, in the nineteenth century two French thinkers, Félicité de Lamennais and Auguste Bonnetty, were condemned by the Church because they underrated human reason applied to faith. Their notion of 'blind' faith was rejected. But at the same time a German named Anton Günther was condemned for wanting to give too much place to reason. He said that the truths of faith must be understood by reason. That would eliminate the obscurity of faith.[1]

So faith should be reasonable but that does not make it totally comprehensible. We have to accept its obscurity. Once again we can make an analogy with the act of loving: when someone tells me he loves me, I can have good reason to believe him but I cannot get absolute proof of the fact. I have to 'accept' that it is true, I have to believe it. It is the same with God. We can say that it is reasonable that there is a God but our will has to accept it if there is to be an act of faith. What is more, and this is the 'crux theologorum', the grace of God acts before, during and after this acceptance. Faith is reasonable even though necessarily obscure (see also chapter 7) and it is this very obscurity that leaves us free in the matter of faith. I can, if I want, *not* believe, and on the other hand I must never believe blindly.

At this point it would be helpful to have a lengthy commentary on the illuminating passage of Paul to the Corinthians:

> Has not God made foolish the wisdom of the world? For since, in the wisdom of God, the world did not know God through wisdom, it pleased God through the folly of what we preach to save those who believe. For Jews demand signs and Greeks seek wisdom, but we preach Christ crucified, a stumbling-block to Jews and folly to Gentiles, but to those who are called, both Jews and Greeks, Christ the power of God and the wisdom of God. For the foolishness of God is wiser than men, and the weakness of God is stronger than men (1 Corinthians 1 : 20-25).

1. Lamennais was condemned in the encyclical *Mirari vos* (1832), Bonnetty in the decree *Indicis* (1855), and Günther in the papal brief *Eximiam tuam* (1857).

41

Obstacles to growth in grace and truth

Why do people find it so difficult to accept Catholicism if, as this book suggests, it is 'so simple'?

I would say, broadly speaking, that there are four main obstacles:

1. the obscurity of faith
2. the problem of evil
3. the lack of true Christian witness in the history of Christianity, especially on the part of churchmen and the institutional Church
4 the life-experience and the psychosomatic make-up of the individual.

Chapter 40 deals with the obscurity of faith and chapter 39 with the problem of evil; there is not much to say about the lack of true Christian witness: the only thing is to make amends and — try to do better. We have all been at fault and, unfortunately, we all continue to be so. By way of excuse, I will just say this: the visible Church is made up of human beings and it is they who give such a poor Christian witness. I say to everyone: "Let him who is without sin" — when he confronts his *own* ideals and his *own* commitments — "let him throw the first stone".

The fourth obstacle is the most subtle. People transfer it to or transform it into one or all of the other three obstacles where it seeks refuge.

Here the variations are really endless. We can become prey to all sorts of psychological tricks. The identification of God with a dictatorial and repressive father is the first which springs to mind. Then there are all the forms of anger (often apparently entirely justifiable) which come from our own experience of life, and this leads to anger with life itself and so with the Creator of life: "I do not want to accept life if it's like this". There are some people who have been so humiliated that it has made them almost incurably proud. There are a million different fears which can turn into pride or rigidity or rejection; there is the faulty religious instruction which leads to prejudices which are in turn easily increased by any of the first three obstacles to faith; and to give an answer to each of those things, we would have to go into the life history of each individual separately. We would need the services of a psychologist of the faith, that is, a spiritual director.

In psychiatry (and also in ordinary medicine), the sick person is cured, not so much by the doctor as by his own inner vitality, by a mainspring being released, setting free the vital resources of the patient himself. Here, also, it is not so much reasoning or human love which overcomes the obstacles but the grace of God which dispels them. As the doctor and psychiatrist are only instruments, here, too, reasoning, good will and someone to talk to are only means to an end. As in medicine, where the first thing necessary is the wish to be cured, and as in psychiatry where it is necessary for the patient to be quite open with the psychiatrist, here, too, the person must be totally open to God. God always respects human liberty.

This journey towards faith is not necessarily a process of auto-suggestion as is often feared, but a thirst for truth, a thirst for the God who pursues and torments us — classically portrayed in Francis Thompson's "The Hound of Heaven" — until we dicover a meaning to life which fits in with the reality we know and experience.

This discovery — which unbelievers call an invention — is the basis of faith and if we are to live honestly, we must make it afresh each day of our lives.

"Fecisti nos ad te, Deus, et inquietum est cor nostrum donec requiescat in te" (You made us for you, O God, and our heart is restless until it rests in you) St Augustine tells us.

42

Growth in grace and human growth

If we want to undertand and get a firm grasp of how grace acts and how one grows in the understanding of divine realities, we can study the apostle Peter.

In the Gospels, Peter is a good, friendly, generous, enthusiastic man, always thrusting himself forward, but he is also fearful, a bungler and unfaithful. (See for example Matthew 14:22-31 where Peter tries to walk on water, the foot-washing in John 13:6-10 and the triple denial of Peter in Matthew, Mark and Luke. Incidentally, these things are for me one of the rational 'proofs' of the truth of the Gospels: what book of 'propaganda' would portray one of its chief heroes in such a way if it were not true?)

Peter's cowardice lasts until Pentecost. Afterwards, having received the Holy Spirit, Peter still has all his human limitations: he is still hasty and a bit naive, and also a bit of a bungler (see the episode with Cornelius and the dispute with Paul), but he becomes wise, prudent, courageous and faithful in a way we should hardly have expected. This account is quite inadequate; in order to understand what I am saying, it is necessary to read the texts in the Gospels (to have an idea of the situation before Pentecost) and in the Acts of the Apostles (after Pentecost).

In a rather different way, we can speak of growth in Jesus, too. But here it is human growth. Jesus' human nature grew and developed in the normal way — to the maximum of human potential, but still normally. (Christ in the crib did *not* cry as infants do, all the while saying to himself: "I know I am God but I have to pretend that I'm a baby". He simply cried.) Already at the age of twelve he knew there was something very special about him — he probably knew he was the Messiah promised to the Hebrews in the Old Testament (see Luke 2:41). But I doubt very much if, as man, he knew much more than that.

43

The Jews and the Messiah

People often ask me if there is still a living faith among the Jews. Here is a little story on the subject which moved me greatly when I was young. My grandmother was a healthy unbeliever who generously helped her neighbours in a society with huge social differences. She was a rich woman and among the other 'good works' she engaged in was a Jewish community project called *La Soupe populaire*, literally a soup kitchen where poor people could get a bowl of soup. One day my grandmother came home furious. At table she said to my mother: "Do you remember Rachel — that woman with seven children and the lazy husband who's always drunk? Well, she's pregnant again. I told her she should get an abortion. If she doesn't, I won't help her anymore. And do you know what she dared to answer me?", my grandmother went on angrily. "You know what she said? 'But, Madame, what if it were the Messiah?' "

44

St Paul

I would very much have liked to know St Peter, and St John perhaps even more, but I don't know if I would have got on with St Paul. I think he would have annoyed me with his fire and zeal. I think I would have found him unpleasant. What is more, they say that he was small and ugly. (The information we have on him and his life — and there is plenty of it — comes to us either from the Acts of the Apostles or from his letters.)

But Paul is the man from whom I have learnt the most theologically (and therefore his is the most vital influence). His letters are more intelligent and more profoundly spiritual than the writing of any other author I know. His superior intelligence led him to understand the consequences of Christianity much more explicitly than the other, less cultured and less reflective apostles — whence the accusation brought against him of having 'invented' Christianity.

His vision of reality, of Christianity, is not only coherent but breathtakingly profound (all or almost all the Letter to the Romans as well as Ephesians 1, Philippians 2 and Colossians 1). He is accused of having narrow ideas, of being a misogynist and a bigot. These are unjust accusations — he was certainly a man of his time, with the limitations of his time, but few have preached liberty and equality more than he did: "There is no longer Jew or Gentile, slave or freeman, male or female, you are all one in Christ Jesus" (Galatians 3 : 28). There is no longer black or white, worker or employer, man or woman, we should say today. And no one has spoken as he did on the supremacy of love:

If I speak in the tongues of men and of angels, but have not love, I am a noisy gong or a clanging cymbal. And if I have prophetic powers, and understand all mysteries and all knowledge, and I have all faith, so as to remove mountains, but have not love, I am nothing. If I give away all I have, and if I deliver my body to be burned, but have not love, I gain nothing. Love is patient and kind; love is not jealous or boastful; it is not arrogant or rude. Love does not insist on its own way; it is not irritable or resentful; it does not rejoice at wrong, but rejoices in the right. Love bears all things, believes all things, hopes all things, endures all things (1 Corinthians 13:17).

45

Difficult decisions

When one has to make a difficult decision, perhaps involving one's life, and one is a Christian, one is in an enviable position. It is almost an instance, if you will, of religion as the 'opium of the people', only that the opium here is a medicine and not a drug, for two reasons: in the first place, because the Christian not only can make use of all human help available but has supernatural help as well; secondly, because even if he does make a mistake, even if he falls into sin, there is always a remedy.

Every Christian is first of all a human being, which means that when he has to make a decision he has first to think it over and use all the human faculties of intelligence, intuition, judgement, etc. Then he will consult with friends who are trusted, wise and competent (old people are often excellent advisers at this point). And thus he should arrive at a possible solution to the problem, a possible decision. So far he has acted as any sensible person would. After this a Christian can — and should — take a further step: submit his decision to the Holy Spirit.

This is done by praying to the Spirit in the following way: "Using my natural capacities and consulting with those able to help me, I have arrived at this decision. I am not completely convinced, but it seems to me the best thing. I will follow it. If it is wrong, may I be shown this before I put the decision into practice".

At the right time, we shall put the decision we have made into practice; perhaps we will have been mistaken but we shall certainly have done all that depended on us. This does *not* mean that we need not bear the consequences of the mistake (otherwise the solution would really be 'opium' in the worst sense) but we will do so with an easy mind because it was not possible to do more than we did do to avoid the mistake.

It also happens that the Holy Spirit lets us know — in time — that our decision is wrong. The thousands of ways this can happen would require a book in itself. Laurens van der Post, in *The Lost World of the Kalahari*,[1] starts chapter 8 with this sentence: "By chance (to use the only phrase we have for describing one of the most significant manifestations of life) that very morning a plane . . .". This 'chance' is one of the ways the Spirit works.

In fact one could say — and Leon Bloy says something similar — that 'chance' is the name lay people give to the Holy Spirit, to Providence (*pace* Jacques Monod). For the Christian, the world is immersed in the Holy Spirit, in Providence; the world is in the Tao (see chapter 46) — or rather when you follow your 'appointed path' in the world, you are in line with the Tao. If you follow the Tao, your decision cannot fail to be the right one. Christ should be the model; it is a question of using all one's human faculties and then opening oneself to the Spirit and going forward.

The second reason why a Christian is in a privileged position when he makes choices is that, even if he makes a mistake, even if he sins, everything can — if he is seeking God — turn out for the good.

Two quotations will illustrate what I mean: the first is St Augustine commenting on St Paul. In chapter 8 of the Letter to the Romans, St Paul says: "We know that in everything God works for good with those who love him" (Romans 8:28). "Even sin", adds St Augustine. This means that even the evil we do, even the mistakes we make (see chapter 64), if we acknowledge and regret them, are turned by God into means of growth. The second is a passage from Manzoni's *The Betrothed*:

> It is one of the peculiar and incommunicable pro-
> perties of the Christian religion, that she can afford
> guidance and repose to all who, under whatever cir-

cumstances, or in whatever exigence, have recourse to her. If there is a remedy for the past, she prescribes it, administers it, and lends light and energy to put it in force, at whatever cost; if there is none, she teaches how to do that effectually and in reality, which the world prescribes proverbially — make a virtue of necessity. She teaches how to continue with discretion what is thoughtlessly undertaken; she inclines the mind to cleave steadfastly to what was imposed upon it by authority; and imparts to a choice which, though rash at the time, is now irrevocable, all the sanctity, all the advisedness, and, let us say it boldly, all the cheerfulness of a lawful calling. Here is a path so constructed that, let a man approach it by what labyrinth or precipice he may, he sets himself, from that moment, to walk in it with security and readiness, and at once begins to draw towards a joyful end.[2]

1. Laurens van der Post, *The Lost World of the Kalahari*, Penguin Books, 1964.
2. Alessandro Manzoni, *I Promessi Sposi* (*The Betrothed*), The Harvard Classics, vol. 21, edited by Charles W. Eliot, 1909.

46

Christianity and the Tao

Taoism is a philosophy/religion of Chinese origin which stems from Lao Tsu who lived about 500 B.C. Taoism has changed a lot in the course of time. In this chapter I am referring to the most ancient collection we have of Taoist sayings, a work ascribed to Lao Tsu, the *Tao Te Ching*.

Reading the *Tao Te Ching*, I found basic Christian concepts which have not only been very little developed in the West but which open up new ways of understanding Christ and therefore Christianity.

I am not trying to present Taoism here or to make comparisons. I only want to encourage people to read the *Tao Te Ching* and try to see how much it is in harmony with Christianity.

The Taoist attitudes which we would call humility and passivity seem particularly interesting to me.

Everyone knows that humility is one of the central virtues of Christianity, but certainly the Christianity we see around us does not appear humble and rarely is humility given a central place in Christian teaching. But it is at the centre of Taoist teaching. Humility is truth; if someone is humble, he is what he is and faces up to things as they are. As a result, a Taoist is poor in spirit just as the Beatitudes say one should be. The Taoist follows the Tao, the Way.

To understand love and grow in love, it seems to me that we need to have the Taoist attitude to creation: don't push, be open and available, be calm; imitate water, which flows where it is easiest to go, allow the world and things to act upon you.

The comparison with passivity is even more striking. We are obsessed by activity; it seems that if we are not *doing* something, we are not *alive*. But the Taoist does *not* do (e.g., *Tao Te Ching* XVI, XXXVII); he is passive and so fully active.

There is a force, a dynamism in things, in reality, in the world, which, if one follows it, if one fits in with it, allows us to develop harmoniously; but if we try to force it, to direct or possess it, it blocks us and causes damage. Christians call this force grace, the Taoists call it the Tao.

People often ask me why Jesus allowed himself to be crucified at the age of thirty-three. "Think how much good he could have done if he had lived another thirty years". We do not perhaps readily agree with this remark, but perhaps we do not immediately see why. A Taoist, on the other hand, would understand at once.

Jesus had to go his own way, follow his Tao; he could not follow the reasoning of the world, however good, nor could he go the way of the world.

In the whole of history, the most powerful action, which changed the world and saved the world, was the passion of Christ.

Death on a cross — that is, by worldly standards, the most passive act imaginable — is, for the Christian, the act of salvation. We are not used to thinking of passivity as strength and power. But the Taoist does, and so does the Gospel; for the Christian, as for the Taoist, it is true to say that in a certain sense the one who wins loses and the one who loses wins. There is a whole theology which needs developing in the light of this truth, and a reading of the *Tao Te Ching* would be a great help. Not that we lack a strong vein of Christian thought along these very lines (e.g., Dionysius the Aeropagite and Master Eckhart): this vein is part of mystical theology, which is rarely talked about.

Many traditions recognize the terrible dangers of power, how it corrupts and distorts one's vision of reality; many parts of the Bible — especially the Gospels and Paul's letters — and the Christian mystical tradition offer solutions similar to those of the Tao, to safeguard us from these dangers.

Power comes from the Tao, that is from the Way, alone; God is the only source of power, so we need to seek him and, having found the way, we need to follow it with patience.

47

Humility

We need to distinguish clearly between humility and humiliation. The Christian virtue is to be humble, not necessarily to seek humiliation.

Humiliation is the result of sin, either one's own or others'. One can endure it and one can also seek it out, but only with the intention of taking others' sins upon oneself (see chapter 55).

Humility, on the other hand, is conformity to the truth. One is what one is, no more no less; and above all, one is a creature. We did *not* create ourselves. Therefore we should be at the disposal of our Creator: "Let it be done to me according to your word" (Luke 1:38), says Mary, the *humble* maiden, but let it be noted, *not* before she has objected and tried to understand (Luke 1:34-37), using her human prerogative, reason. Humility, faithfulness, always presuppose obedience, but never blind obedience.

In the Old Testament we have the figures of the *anawim*, the poor people of God, God's favourites. They are also the suffering servants, types of the Suffering Servant, the Christ, the poor and humble man *par excellence*.

As it is rightly said that all sins begin and end with pride, so one could say that all virtues are founded on humility.

PART V

Still more thoughts

This fifth part consists of technical information; it is an attempt to clear up certain misunderstandings and to unravel certain problems. It is didactic at times, but this is necessary if we are to clarify our ideas.

While Part IV sought to fill in the mosaic, this part aims at a greater precision, a 'firing' of the tiles which have already been laid.

48

Words used in theology

There are many technical words used in theology which are still in use today and which the magisterium of the Church insists on using, but which irritate and confuse many people (e.g. 'substance', 'nature', 'person', 'transubstantiation', etc.).

I do not believe the Church attaches any magical power to these words, but the concepts underlying them are so difficult to understand that the use of particular words to express them is the fruit of a long and laborious historical process. Having decided on the suitability of a word — for example the Trinity is three 'persons' in one 'nature', and Christ is one 'person' in two 'natures' — the Church fears that the use of other words would leave even more room for error and confusion.

Out of prudence, therefore, we need to have valid and well-considered reasons before we reject the old terminology in favour of the new. (I, for example, would prefer not to use the word 'transubstantiation' — even if it is entirely accurate theologically — in speaking of the Eucharist, because so many theologians in recent times have pointed out its limitations, but I would certainly use the words 'person' and 'nature' in speaking of the Trinity.)

49

The Fathers of the Church

The Fathers of the Church are the Christians, often bishops but not always, often saints but not always, whom the Church numbers among its masters and whose writings and preaching have come down to us.

They are generally divided into periods: the Fathers of the first, second, third or fourth century, etc., or into geographical areas: Alexandrians, Cappadocians (present-day Turkey), Africans, etc., or according to the language in which they wrote or preached: Greek, Latin, Syriac, etc.

Here are some names: Origen, Clement, Athanasius (Alexandrians); Basil, Gregory of Nyssa (Cappadocians); Cyprian, Augustine (Africans); Athenagoras, John Chrysostom (Greeks); Jerome, Ambrose, Gregory the Great (Latins).

Naturally these categories overlap: Ambrose and Basil are fourth century, Origen and Basil are Greek Fathers, Ambrose and Augustine are Latin Fathers.

Generally, only those who lived up to the eighth century are called Fathers. But it is an elastic term and sometimes a writer like St Bernard (twelfth century) is called a Father of the Church.

The writings of the Fathers were collected in the last century by an extraordinary person: the Abbé Migne. The Latin 'Migne', which incorporates the works originally written in Latin, runs to 221 volumes and the Greek 'Migne' has 161 volumes.

At present there are critical editions of nearly all the Fathers, translated into many different languages.

50

Doctrinal notes

Not all theological statements have the same value. You can be a Catholic without believing everything a bishop or pope says.

How can one assess the value of various statements? From the doctrinal rating given to the statement in question (rather like examination marks: A, B, C, Pass, Fail, etc.). So what we call 'doctrinal notes' are grades given to theological statements in order to establish their value.

Different theologians give different lists: I will give one of these lists, with examples. We shall have nine ratings or, if you like, nine grades.

1. *A doctrine of divine faith.* E.g., the man Jesus of Nazareth of whom we read in the New Testament is the Messiah desired and awaited by the Hebrews in the Old Testament.

This rating is given to statements which can be directly inferred by reading the sacred Scriptures.

2. *A doctrine of defined Catholic faith.* E.g., Christ is the Incarnation of the second Person of the Blessed Trinity.

This rating is given to statements which can be deduced in part from the Bible, on which Christian tradition has then reflected and which the Church has later solemnly defined in ecumenical councils or by a pope speaking *ex cathedra* (up to the present time, this second form of definition has only happened twice in the history of the Church — see chapter 61).

3. *A doctrine of Catholic faith deduced from the ordinary magisterium of the Church — in Latin: ex magisterio ordinario.* E.g., the universal motherhood of

115

Mary, Mother of the Church. This rating is given to beliefs currently held by the Church and which have been held 'semper et ubique' (see chapter 59), by many of the Fathers, bishops and popes. Sometimes there is a liturgical feast as well (as in the case of the example given), but these beliefs have never been solemnly defined either by an ecumenical council or by a pope *ex cathedra*.

4. *Doctrine close to the Faith.* E.g., All men are in some sense members of the Church.

This rating is given to statements which, though of long standing, have needed later definition and clarification and will not be accepted by everyone, at least not in the form expressed.

5. *Certain doctrine.* E.g., Christ, the Son of God, had ten fingers.

A 'certain' doctrine is derived from a doctrine of divine faith or of defined faith, added to a process of reasoning. In this case it is a defined doctrine that Christ the Son of God is true and perfect man. So, as a perfect man has ten fingers, therefore Christ had ten fingers. This point, which hardly seems important in the example given, becomes crucial when, for example, people ask if Christ had a human intellect, that is, an intellect which develops and grows with age (see chapter 42).

6. *A doctrine of ecclesiastical faith.* E.g., St Francis of Assisi is really a saint.

This rating is given to affirmations solemnly proclaimed by the Church but which are not directly concerned with the fundamentals of the faith.

7. *Common doctrine.* E.g., Mary, the Mother of Jesus, never committed even the slightest sin.

This rating is given to generally accepted doctrine about which, however, there is quite a lot of disagreement. In this case, some theologians would have no difficulty in saying, for example, that Mary lost patience at times (even with Jesus himself; see Luke 2 : 48), and therefore she committed venial sin. But the majority, basing their argument on the doctrine of faith that Mary was free from original sin, agree with popular piety in holding that Mary never sinned at all.

8. *More common doctrine.* E.g., defensive warfare is legitimate.

9. *Less common doctrine.* E.g., after the introduction of nuclear weapons, war is never legitimate.

These two ratings are self-explanatory. With the passage of time, a more common (commonly held doctrine) can become less common and the less common can become common or even close to the faith or of faith.

That is why it is so interesting to study the history of the development of certain dogmas and definitions. Dogmas are formulations of truths held by the Church to be basic and permanent, for example, that God is one and triune. By studying the development of dogma, one comes to understand how, historically and theologically, the Church has arrived at certain truths of the faith.

The coherence and logic of 'revealed' doctrines which have appeared over the centuries and the way in which people and the Church have accepted them and incorporated them (e.g., the development of certain ideas in sacred Scripture — see chapters 12 and 13) impress by their lucidity and profundity.

To be a Catholic, that is, in full communion with the Church of Rome, one must at least accept the affirmations which come under the first two categories. From the third onwards, it is permissible to dissent.

Obviously, the first requisite for disagreement is humility on the part of the one who dissents. One should try to be well-informed, to know exactly what the belief involves, to know the history of the doctrine, etc. The less important the rating, the freer one is to dissent. It is heretical to dissent from affirmations which fall into the first two categories and rash to dissent from the ordinary magisterium.

In conclusion: many statements generally believed to be an essential part of the Catholic faith are not so in fact. Every Christian should know about doctrinal ratings in order to know what he should believe if he wants to call himself a Catholic. Many people, I think, would be in for surprises, both good and bad. Theology is not for theologians only but for everybody.

The essential sources for such a study are: (1) The Bible; (2) The texts of the ecumenical councils; (3) The writings of the Church Fathers (see chapter 49); and (4) The liturgical books, past and present, of the East and West.

51

Faith and reason

In the minds of many people, faith and reason are opposites. But for the Christian they are complementary.

Faith deals precisely with the things we *cannot* understand completely and which we shall never be able to understand completely, because they concern God and are therefore 'bigger than us', incomprehensible; they are beyond the reaches of our language, our terminology and our framework. But this does not imply that the things which faith offers to our belief are not reasonable, that faith can contradict our reason and experience.

Reason, on the other hand, deals with the things which are on our level or those 'smaller' than us.

The finest explanation of why faith and reason cannot contradict one another but are, rather, complementary, is, I think, that set forth by the First Vatican Council in 1870, when the controversy between faith and reason was at its most intense.

> Although it is true that faith is above reason, nevertheless there can never be real disagreement between faith and reason: because the same God, who reveals mysteries and infuses faith, has given the human soul the light of reason; indeed God cannot deny himself, nor can truth ever contradict itself. So . . . when . . . the illusion of such a contradiction arises: either the dogmas of the faith have not been understood and expounded according to the understanding of the Church, or the opinions which contradict the faith are erroneously held to be rational. (Vatican Council I, *Dei Filius*, chap. 4)

52

The Trinity

The Unity and the Trinity of God is one of the two 'mysteries' of the faith; the other is the Incarnation. A mystery is something which we cannot understand.

We have already seen how, logically, God cannot be 'understood' by human beings. The lesser can never understand the greater.

But this should not stop us from trying to understand the mystery as much as we are able, and we should at least be able to show how and why what we have said is not absurd. Among other things, it is bordering on heresy to say, "I believe because it is absurd" — God is never absurd. (See chapter 51.)

Various theologians have used various reasoning and examples to help us to understand the Trinity. I like St Augustine's:

If I think of myself, I tend to form a more or less vague mental image of myself in a certain place or in a certain situation. Now, when God thinks of himself, his thought is so powerful that it generates another person. (Why these two persons are called 'Father' and 'Son' should be studied by religious historians, psychologists, sociologists, etc. Christ also called the Father 'father' but he is a very special kind of 'father'.)

When God thinks about himself, then, he generates God; but they are two persons in one nature, to use traditional terminology, not two Gods but one God. (My image of myself when I think of myself does not make two of me.) The second stage is when these two persons contemplate one another with love. I, too, can think about (contemplate) and love myself.

When the Father contemplates the Son and the Son contemplates the Father, they love each other so much that they 'breathe out' the third persons, the Holy Spirit. (The most famous controversy between the churches of Rome and Constantinople — between Catholic and Orthodox Christians — was technically on precisely this point, that is, the addition of 'and the Son' to the Nicene Creed. Catholics say that the breathing out of the Holy Spirit comes from the Father *and* from the Son, being the fruit of a mutual love. The Orthodox, on the other hand, say that it comes from the Father *through* the Son. Is this casuistry or a point of fundamental importance?)

So the Trinity is one God who, knowing himself, generates the Son and, loving himself, breathes out the Holy Spirit. A single nature in three persons.

The action of the three persons in creation and in the plan of salvation is also very interesting. I will mention a few points: it is the Son who became incarnate (the Word, the one made known) and not the Father or the Spirit. But at Pentecost it was the Spirit, Love, who came down on the apostles, who was sent from the Father and from the Son in order to give life to the Church and to every man. It is the Spirit which every person has within if he or she is 'in the grace of God'.

But we can also say that God became incarnate (the Son is *also* God) and that we have God within us (the Spirit is *also* God). It is clear that the language is used in an analogical way, improperly, as is always the case when we speak of God.

Hundreds of books have been written about these things, but perhaps the most beautiful thing written is the Creed (technically called the 'Symbol') ascribed to St Athanasius (an Alexandrian Father who died in 373) but probably written in the fifth century:

> Whosover will be saved: before all things it is necessary that he hold the Catholic Faith. . . .
> And the Catholic Faith is this: that we worship one

God in Trinity, and Trinity in Unity; neither confounding the Persons: nor dividing the substance.

For there is one Person of the Father, another of the Son: and another of the Holy Spirit;

But the Godhead of the Father, of the Son and of the Holy Spirit, is all one: the glory equal, the majesty co-eternal.

Such as the Father is, such is the Son: and such is the Holy Spirit.

The Father uncreated, the Son uncreated: and the Holy Spirit uncreated.

The Father incomprehensible, the Son incomprehensible: and the Holy Spirit incomprehensible.

The Father eternal, the Son eternal: and the Holy Spirit eternal.

And yet they are not three eternals: but one eternal.

As also there are not three incomprehensibles, nor three uncreated: but one uncreated, and one incomprehensible.

So likewise the Father is almighty, the Son is almighty: and the Holy Spirit almighty.

And yet they are not three almighties: but one almighty.

So the Father is God, the Son is God: and the Holy Spirit is God.

And yet they are not three Gods but one God.

So likewise the Father is Lord, the Son Lord: and the Holy Spirit Lord.

And yet not three Lords: but one Lord.

For as we are compelled by Christian truth to acknowledge every Person by himself to be God and Lord,

So we are forbidden by the Catholic religion to speak of three Gods or three Lords.

The Father is made of none: neither created nor begotten.

The Son is of the Father alone: not made, nor created, but begotten.

The Holy Spirit is of the Father and of the Son:

neither made, nor created, nor begotten, but pro-
ceeding from them both.

So there is one Father, not three Fathers; one Son,
not three Sons: one Holy Spirit, not three Holy
Spirits.

And in this Trinity none comes before or after
another: none is greater or less than another; but
the whole three Persons are co-eternal together:
and co-equal.

So that in all things, as has already been said, the
Unity in Trinity and the Trinity is Unity is to be
worshipped. . . .

Furthermore is it necessary to everlasting salvation:
that he also rightly believe in the Incarnation of our
Lord Jesus Christ.

For the right faith is, that we believe and confess: that
our Lord Jesus Christ, the Son of God, is God and
Man.

God of the substance of the Father, begotten before
the world: and Man of the substance of his
Mother, born in the world.

Perfect God and perfect Man. . . .

And there follow similar clarifications which are more concerned with Christology than with the Trinity. After reading this it is even easier to understand why we tend not
to change theological terms (see chapter 48).

53

Mary

When we think of the place of Mary in Catholic teaching, we do *not* have to think of the great mother goddess of so many religions, nor of other goddesses like Diana of Ephesus, as so many people tend to do.

Certainly these or similar interpretations of Marian doctrine have always been a great temptation to Christians. It is most interesting to see that in the Index of Prohibited Books[1] we have a really large number of books containing excessive devotion to Mary, in which she tends to become a 'great mother'. The Church condemns them outright. The Church's devotion to Mary is linked to the fact, for example, that Jesus took flesh of her flesh, but it is even more strongly linked to the figure of Mary as the creature who made herself most available to God in his plan of redemption. She is really a model, almost as much as her Son is (see chapter 22). She is a model of humility (see chapter 47), a model of patience.

Mary is *not* a saviour, she is *not* a redeemer, but she is mother of the Saviour, mother of the Redeemer, and therefore in a very real sense she is the Mother of God. Like all the other saints, Mary intercedes for us (see chapter 55) and her intercession, because of her role in salvation history, is held to be specially powerful.

What is more, Mary has completed the human journey and has been taken up into heaven (see chapter 54); she is still our model there and with her Son, our forerunner.

---

1. A list of books compiled by the Holy Office, which a Catholic could not read without due permission up until the 1960's, when the prohibition was lifted as being antiquated and counter-productive.

54

The Assumption of Mary into Heaven

Whatever people may think, the Church — doctrinally at least — has always upheld earthly values and the value of the body. Against the Manicheans (see chapter 66), she has always held that matter is good and the body is good. What we see and touch, the bodies we love, are not 'maya' as the Indians would say, they are not just illusion, but they are things to respect and love, being destined for eternity. The body is made for 'heaven'.

This is the context into which we have to put the dogma of the Assumption. The dogma of the Assumption of Mary was proclaimed on November 1, 1950, the outcome of a long history. It is one of the only two dogmas that a pope has proclaimed *ex cathedra* (see chapter 61), the other being the Immaculate Conception of Mary, proclaimed by Pius IX in 1854.

The liturgical feast of the Assumption of Mary into heaven is of very long standing in the churches of both East and West. In the East it was combined with the Dormition of Mary, which affirmed that before entering paradise Mary fell asleep but did not die.

Religious art depicting Mary's Assumption is very widespread *'semper et ubique'* (see chapter 59). If the dogma was not proclaimed before, it was because of dissenting voices of great authority in the tradition.

Pope Pius XII, having consulted all the bishops in the world as well as all the theological faculties, proclaimed it in 1950.

At that time, theologians were much preoccupied with earthly realities in an effort to counteract the excessive attention given to the spirit to the detriment of the body, both within and without the Church, during and after the Second World War.

There was a tendency to exalt the spiritual and to denigrate the corporal. Pius XII — certainly not an excessively 'corporal' pope — in his bull of proclamation, lays great stress on the body and its eternal destiny, thus reaffirming the value of all terrestrial realities.

55

The Communion of Saints

One of the most consoling doctrines of the Church is the Communion of Saints.

The saints, in the language of the New Testament, are all the baptized (see also chapter 26). But in this doctrine we are thinking more of the so-called Church Triumphant, that is, the dead, now risen, who are in Paradise (see chapter 25). They are already united to God and by this bond of love we also are bound in some way, here on earth (naturally, only if we freely open ourselves to it). The saints are already 'full' members of the Body of Christ; we are still 'part' members, still in preparation, so to speak — in via, as the technical term is, that is, 'on the way', but we are linked to them by prayer, devotion and also affection if we have known them on earth. It is in this context that we should understand devotion and prayer to the saints. The love between God and the saints is a love which circulates like blood, and from that blood we too can obtain nourishment (see the marvellous Greater Litany of the Saints).

This doctrine illustrates one of the basic divergencies between Christianity and Hinduism, although it is not the most striking point of contrast.

In Hinduism, where salvation is a strictly personal matter, there is no place for the circulation of love, which often involves taking responsibility for another. (To intercede for us — which is what the saints do — also means to be in some way responsible for us.)

To illustrate this divergence, I quote here a passage from Saverpalli Radhakrishnan, a prominent Indian philosopher who was also President of India and represents one of the high points of modern Indian thought:

A just God cannot refuse to any man that which he has earned. The past guilt cannot be wiped away by the atoning suffering of an outward substitute. Guilt cannot be transferred. It must be atoned for through the sorrow entailed by self-conquest. God cannot be bought over and sin cannot be glossed over.[1]

This is obviously at variance with one of the central tenets of Christian doctrine which is the expiatory death of Christ, that Christ died for us.

Under the *lex talionis*, "an eye for an eye and a tooth for a tooth", the law of justice (see chapter 13), in a world where there was nothing but justice, guilt *could not* be transferred. But under the law of love, it can be.

The Communion of Saints can only be effective if Christ's law is in force, the law of love.

1. Saverpalli Radhakrishnan, *The Hindu View of Life*, George Allen and Unwin, 1961, p. 54.

56

Infant baptism

Some people would like to postpone the baptism of children until they are fifteen to twenty years of age, in order to leave them 'free' to choose.

I would like to make two objections to this view. The first, not a very serious one, but which has a certain weight, is that between fifteen and twenty years of age, young people have to wrestle with three acute problems: (a) What sort of work am I going to do? What am I going to do with my life? (The choice of a profession, of a university, etc.) (b) All the problems connected with their budding sexuality. (c) The problems of leaving home and family (with all the clashes with parents that such a decision often involves). Knowing that in order to grow up they must 'go away', cut loose, leave the nest, but also knowing that to stay at home gives strength and security, and having to choose between the two.

These things make these particular years — which I feel are wrongly called 'the best years of one's life' — a very difficult time indeed.

To add to all that the problem of choosing or rejecting baptism seems to me *very* cruel. To be free to choose one's religion, one could postpone confirmation — which is also the sacrament where one accepts one's own baptism. One could (should) *choose* to be confirmed, *choose* to be a witness to Christ; confirmation therefore should be administered at an older age than usually happens.

The second objection is more strictly theological: if baptism confers grace, the life of Christ and the life of God, why refuse it to an infant?

Grace will become effective at the first moment that the

child needs it; how can we judge when a child will need it? So the argument of 'choice' is spurious: our parents certainly don't ask us if we want to be born (and what an imposition *that* is!); they give us life; if we don't like it, we can throw it away (by suicide). Why not also give us Life? We can always throw it away.

57

The symbols of baptism

There is a tremendous wealth of symbolism in all the sacraments; nearly all the sacraments, however, have pre-Christian origins.[1]

The sacraments, like much of what we meet in the teaching and life of the Church, are rooted in everyday reality, in the life and in the history of human kind. Everything is prefigured, foreshadowed.

The Church, Christianity, continues and develops those parts of creation, those parts of the world as we know it, which can be continued and developed, and it takes up and transforms whatever can be taken up and transformed. God is one, so the natural and supernatural, creation and re-creation, that is, the intervention of God in time and space, are adapted to one another and complement one another. For example, baptism as a rite of purification and initiation is very ancient, and such baptisms are full of symbolism: just think of all the symbolism of water: it washes, nourishes, fertilizes, fosters growth, floods, drowns, destroys, etc. Now baptism includes all this: it nourishes, fertilizes and causes the good to grow; it washes, destroys, drowns and floods out evil, sin, the serpent, Satan. Similar considerations could be applied to all the sacraments.

---

1. See the remarkable essay by Hugo Rahner, 'The Christian Mystery and the Pagan Mysteries' (1944), in *The Mysteries: Papers from the Eranos Yearbooks*, Bollingen Series XXX, 2.

58

Ex opere operato

Speaking of the sacraments (see chapter 27) we said that
they do not 'take' in those people who are not disposed to
receive them. But the Church teaches that the sacraments
act *ex opere operato*, that is, they are effective in themselves. What does this mean, and how do we reconcile these
two apparently contradictory statements? The first seems to
make the efficacy of the sacraments dependent on the goodwill of the person receiving them, the second smacks of
magic.

To start with, we can say that Christ instituted the sacraments to help — to save — human beings and that the
Church, the Body of Christ, was made for man and not
man for the Church. Therefore the 'economy of the sacraments', as it is called in theology — the functioning of the
sacraments if you like — is always to our advantage, to
help us, to make us grow, and it cannot be subject to legal-
isms or arbitrary limitations.

When we have rigid provisions for the practice and
administration of the sacraments, it is in order to protect
those who receive them. When those who receive them are
in good faith *and* we have the basic minimum of actions
prescribed by the Church to make it a sacrament, then the
sacrament is always valid.

It is obvious that the minimum of external actions will
vary from sacrament to sacrament, since the context and
role of each sacrament varies in the life of each recipient.

Here are two examples: the first illustrates the primary
importance of the person who *receives* the sacrament: if
anyone, even a great sinner who is not even baptized,
baptizes someone with the wish of carrying out the

intention of the Church, then it is a real and efficacious baptism if the person baptized is disposed to receive it (this is also true if one baptizes a child). Anyone, then, solely by being a human being, can bring another person into the Body of Christ and everything is done to encourage it. The sacrament is effective *not* because the person administering it is good or worthy — far from it — but it is efficacious *ex opere operato*, that is, because the action has been carried out. It is always Christ, and not the one who administers them, who acts in the sacraments.

The second example shows how the Church protects a person in the sacraments; it concerns the discipline of the sacrament of marriage. Towards the end of the Council of Trent in 1563, there was talk of the sacrament of marriage, and in particular of clandestine marriages. At that time, church marriages were not subject to the same discipline as they are now, and too many men deceived women into thinking that they were married and then deserted them. The decree *Tametsi* established that in order for a marriage to be valid, it must be witnessed by the parish priest of the woman, or his delegate — otherwise it is invalid. Thus women were protected. But this legislation was not entirely restrictive; the interests of those who were to receive the sacrament were safeguarded and the following case shows how: if an engaged couple are on a desert island with no prospect of having a priest or anyone else to witness their marriage vows for a period of about a month, a simple reciprocal 'Yes' constitutes a valid and legitimate sacrament of marriage.

59

Revelation

We said in chapter 11 that God reveals himself to human beings, he makes himself known to the extent to which we can perceive him and understand him. But how can the Church be sure of what has been revealed? How can it know that it is not mistaken when it proposes a doctrine as revealed?

To understand this, it is necessary to see: (a) what is the fundamental guarantee of revelation in the eyes of the Church; (b) what are the sources of revelation; and (c) how one determines the degree of certainty for each affirmation and what are the criteria of validity.

To these questions we can answer that:

1. The Church's guarantee is the Holy Spirit, God himself. On the Day of Pentecost, the Holy Spirit came down on the apostles who were gathered in Jerusalem (Acts 2: 1-4).

Christian tradition says that on that day the Church was born. In fact, before his death Christ said to the apostles: "These things I have spoken to you, while I am still with you. But the Counsellor, the Holy Spirit, whom the Father will send in my name, he will teach you all things, and bring to your remembrance all that I have said to you" (John 14:25-26 and again in John 16:12-15). And so it was.

Now, even today, the Church believes that the Holy Spirit is with her and continues to be the means whereby revelation is correctly interpreted.

2. It is generally said that there are four sources of revelation: the sacred Scriptures, the Church Fathers, the magisterium and the liturgy.

It is clear that Sacred Scriptures — the Bible — of which God is the 'author' in the sense described in chapter 9, is the primary source of revelation. It is from there that we learn how God revealed himself to the Hebrews, how he entered their history — and ours too — and then came to earth in the person of Jesus of Nazareth.

But this revelation, as we have seen, is not perceived, nor understood, nor received by men all at once, in all its depth and with all its intricacies. The Church — all the faithful in time and space, that is, in history — the Church, step by step, is ever perceiving more and deepening its understanding.

Down the ages, Christians, confronting the events of life and history, reflecting on the Scriptures in a spirit of prayer and aided by the Spirit, do not discover *new* truths but truths which were not previously perceived and understood.

The Fathers of the Church (see chapter 49) are those who completed an important part of this work of reflection: which is why they are called another source of revelation — perhaps it would be better to say a source of explanation of revelation — and they form part of the Church's tradition, of what the Church 'carries with it'.

The faithful, in their meditation and prayer, aided by the Holy Spirit, can also discover these truths or the connection between different truths and express them in prayers and hymns. Their prayers and hymns, inspired by the Spirit, are included (when the whole Church sees fit) in the official prayer of the Church, the liturgy. It is in this way that the liturgy, too, can become a source of revelation.

Finally, the magisterium of the Church (the bishops in their writing and preaching) fulfils the same task, and when a doctrine has really emerged as sure and has been tested, they set it forth as official doctrine in the regional councils, or, more solemnly, as dogma in the ecumenical (worldwide) councils or through the pope (see chapter 61).

3. The degree of certainty a Catholic should attribute to any one of these doctrines can be measured by the theological rating which can be given to it (see chapter 50).

To discover whether a doctrine is truly revealed, that is, if its discovery is inspired by the Holy Spirit and is not merely a pious wish or the immediate product of an historico-social situation, the magisterium of the Church has from ancient times used two criteria. Doctrine should be proposed: (a) *semper et ubique,* "always and everywhere"; and (b) *eodem sensu, eademque sententia,* "in the same sense and with the same interpretation", that is, it must be consistent with other doctrines (without contradiction).

The first criterion tells us that in order to be accepted as revealed, a doctrine should have been accepted by Christians at different times and in different places. If it is just one particular Church in one particular place which accepts a doctrine, it is improbable that it is revealed, since it is not 'always and everywhere'. Thus a number of the Fathers (for example Origen, Tertullian, etc.) at one time or another in their lives held doctrines which the Church now judges as heretical. Because of this, the testimony of some of the Fathers of the Church is more important than that of others. St Irenaeus of Lyon, for instance, was a disciple in Smyrna (now Turkey) of Polycarp, who in his turn had probably known St John the Apostle. Then Irenaeus went to Rome where he met Pope Eleuterius and subsequently became bishop of Lyon in France. He wrote a lot, paying great attention to what the first Christians had said, and he was familiar with the doctrines taught by the churches of Asia, Rome and France because he had heard them at first hand. So St Irenaeus is conversant with teaching 'everywhere'.

The second criterion tells us that in order to be accepted as revealed, a doctrine should be consistent with all the others: God cannot contradict himself (see chapter 51). If a proposed doctrine obviously contradicts other accepted doctrines, it will be rejected by the Church. Now here are two examples to make these ideas clearer:

In the First Letter to the Corinthians (15:29) in a context which does not concern us here, St Paul refers to a usage of the church of Corinth of which there is no trace anywhere else. St Paul merely mentions it, without passing judgment. At Corinth, people were baptized 'for the dead', that is, if a relative died without having been baptized, one could be baptized in the place of that relative. The pre-occupation of the Corinthians is obvious: since in order to be saved, it was necessary to be incorporated into Christ, and only baptism does this, it was necessary to incorporate one's dead relatives into Christ in some way. The baptism of desire (see chapter 26) was not yet a defined doctrine, so people were 'baptized for the dead'. This practice, confined to one Church only, not in force *semper et ubique*, very soon fell into disuse in spite of the fact that even St Paul did not condemn it.

The second example also concerns baptism: St Augustine, during the Pelagian controversy (see chapter 66), rightly maintaining that it was not possible to be saved without the grace of Christ, taught in practice that children who died without baptism therefore went to hell. This doctrine contradicted two fundamental doctrines of theology: that God is just and that God wishes to save all men (1 Timothy 2: 3-4). So the Church rejected it, not directly or explicitly (out of respect for St Augustine), but it is well known (and it was well known even then) that the last chapter of the *Indiculus*, an important Church document of the fifth century, had intended to speak of this problem. The document says that it does not wish to speak of certain difficult questions, neither to condemn certain points of view, nor even less to approve them. The problem of children who die without baptism was left in suspense.

60

The Church as a society

One of the hardest ideas for the modern mind to accept is that of the necessity for a visible, structured Church which is therefore necessarily a centre of power and almost inevitably authoritarian, powerful and part of the establishment.

A serious exposition and discussion of the problem lie outside the scope of this book but it is necessary to mention a few points.

Human beings, who need to organize their perceptions in order to see reality (our brain does this when it receives and synthetizes the perceptions of our five senses), who need to organize their ideas into language in order to understand and communicate them, also need external structures in order to live in society. This is true in social life, in politics as well as in religion. Christ knows this and as he left the visible sacraments to satisfy our need to see and touch, he also left a visible structure, which is the Church. For man, a visible Church is a necessity.

But pride, human greed, ambition, fear and the thirst for power have more than once obscured — and still obscure — what should be the image of Christ expressed by the Church.

But — and this is the real miracle — in spite of all this, the Church is still very alive and is still a place where goodness and holiness can very frequently be found. The Holy Spirit keeps the Church young and vitalizes her, while men make her seem old, betraying her and misrepresenting her. It is for this reason that (as John XXIII reminded us at the Second Vatican Council) *"Ecclesia semper est reformanda"*, the Church must always be in a process of reformation, or rejuvenation. In this connection, I remember how struck I was during the sessions of the Second Vatican Council; here were gathered together two thousand men, all bishops, certainly the great majority of them good and upright, but not particularly brilliant or especially prepared to confront the modern world, being their average age fairly high, yet these men produced documents of extraordinary depth, with a great breadth of vision, extremely wide-ranging, truly prophetic (for example, the pastoral constitution on The Church in the Modern World). This 'society' is indwelt by the Spirit but it has to be a visible, organized society, as are all human societies, even if there is a risk that this visibility and this organization may misrepresent and obscure its role and its mission.

The Second Vatcan Council insisted on the idea of the Church as the people of God: as such, it does not consist merely of the pope and the bishops but of all the baptized. However, as in any human society, there are people at the top; in the Church we have the magisterium, that is, the pope and the bishops, who in their turn are informed and backed by the theologians and by all the faithful (see chapter 61 on infallibility), inspired by the Holy Spirit.

61

Infallibility

Infallibility is a word which causes many negative reactions. After all that has been said, however, it should be clear that for a Catholic, the Church, the Body of Christ, infused with the Holy Spirit, is infallible. It is the *whole* Church that is infallible: "The body of the faithful as a whole, anointed as they are by the Holy One, cannot err in matters of belief. Thanks to the supernatural sense of the faith which characterizes the People as a whole, it manifests this unerring quality when 'from the bishops down to the last member of the laity', it shows universal agreement in matters of faith and morals" (Vatican Council II, *Lumen Gentium* 2:12).

Now, as we have seen, the Church on earth cannot but be a visible society (see chapter 60), and a visible society has a head. Infallibility therefore finds expression first in the whole people of God, but more explicitly and particularly in the bishops, the leaders of the various local churches gathered together in an ecumenical council, and, finally, in the pope alone when he makes a solemn pronouncement *ex cathedra*, that is, from the 'seat' of Peter, the visible head of the Church after the death of Jesus.

This doctrine, developed over a long period, is opposed by other Christians (Orthodox and Protestant) and was defined and clarified by the First and Second Vatican Councils.

Only twice has the Pope spoken solemnly *ex cathedra*: Pius IX in proclaiming the dogma of the Immaculate Conception of Mary in 1854, and Pius XII in proclaiming the Assumption in 1950 (see chapter 54). That these two popes and the whole Church were aware that their infallibility was based on that of the entire Church, vitalized by the Holy Spirit, is obvious from a material fact: in the entrance to St Peter's basilica in Rome there are many marble plaques recording these two proclamations. There are many of them because the two popes wanted to publish the names of the numerous bishops who, in the name of their church — or diocese, as it is called nowadays — had agreed to the proclamation and, in many cases, even requested it.

The Pope is certainly infallible 'on his own' but this pre-supposes his being supported by the Holy Spirit and by the whole Church. The Pope as an individual is no more in direct communication with God than any other individual.

It can also be said that even an infallibly proclaimed dogma can be better understood, further clarified and more profoundly interpreted by the Church in the course of the ages. An infallibly defined dogma is an expression of a truth in human terms, it is not some magic divine formula.

62

Original sin

The Church teaches that every human being is born with original sin and that it is only the grace of Christ which saves us from this sin.

This dogma appears not only strange but also unjust. To help understand it, let us consider the following:

1. Many peoples have the idea that we are all born with sin, defects and a certain responsibility. Primitive legends in Africa, South America, Malaysia, Indonesia and Australia, try to explain this. Hindus and Buddhists believe that one is born with one's *karma*, that is, the weight of all the sins of past lives from which one must seek redemption in this life. The Greeks believed that it was fate, which was laid upon a person at birth and from which there was no escape. Oedipus *had* to kill his father and marry his mother. It was the sins of Laius which fell upon his sons. The Christian believes that we are born with original sin, an imperfection which makes us incapable of fulfilling our destiny alone, unable to save ourselves on our own. Myths, legends, karma, fate, original sin. A great part of humanity is aware of the imperfection in each one of us.

2. For Christians, original sin is a split, a crack, in every person born. People often speak of a stain or shadow, but a fault or crack seems to me to give a better idea. I always think of the San Andreas Fault. This is a fault in the earth's crust which runs from Alaska to California. This fault causes the earthquakes which destroyed San Francisco and which keep recurring. Each one of us is born with a similar fault, a cleavage between what we should (would like to) be and what we are in fact: we lack unity. St Augustine says that we are wounded in our nature and if this wound is not healed, we cannot develop harmoniously and completely.

142

3. The Genesis story, which is a myth in the sense we described in chapter 10, that is, 'truer' than the reality we know, seeks to explain this sin and does so in a brilliant way. Let us listen to it:

> Now the serpent was more subtle than any other wild creature that the Lord God had made. He said to the woman, "Did God say, 'You shall not eat of any tree of the garden'?" And the woman said to the serpent, "We may eat of the fruit of the trees of the garden; but God said, 'You shall not eat of the fruit of the tree which is in the midst of the garden, neither shall you touch it, lest you die". But the serpent said to the woman, "You will not die. For God knows that when you eat of it your eyes will be opened, and you will be like God, knowing good and evil". So when the woman saw that the tree was good for food, and that it was a delight to the eyes, and that the tree was to be desired to make one wise, she took of its fruit and ate; and she also gave some to her husband, and he ate. Then the eyes of both were opened, and they knew that they were naked; and they sewed fig leaves together and made themselves aprons. And they heard the sound of the Lord God walking in the garden in the cool of the day, and the man and his wife hid themselves from the presence of the Lord God among the trees of the garden. But the Lord God called to the man, and said to him, "Where are you?" And he said, "I heard the sound of thee in the garden, and I was afraid, because I was naked; and I hid myself". He said, "Who told you that you were naked? Have you eaten of the tree of which I commanded you not to eat?" The man said, "The woman whom thou gavest to be with me, she gave me fruit of the tree, and I ate". Then the Lord God said to the woman, "What is this that you have done?" The woman said, "The serpent beguiled me, and I ate" (Genesis 3: 1-13).

Here we find death, entropy, non-growth — ice, darkness, fear, independence, loneliness — all the things we have already discussed in connection with what happens when love is lacking and there is nothing but pride. If we cut ourselves off from God, death follows. Not so, says the serpent, then you will be like gods, you will know what good and evil are; you yourselves will be the source of knowing and willing, the source will no longer be someone else: God. You will be in-dependent, you will be autonomous.

If we seek to achieve our autonomy 'by force' (see chapter 29) and not by love, we find loneliness, nakedness, division and death, because through pride, egoism and fear we cut ourselves off from the source of life.

If on the other hand we seek our freedom by binding ourselves to Christ, being incorporated into him, having the courage to love — and any love is a free bond or a bound freedom — then we find salvation and life.

Our inborn and just desire for autonomy becomes freedom through our adherence to Christ. Christ saves us from the wrong sort of autonomy, from the pride and loneliness which are the result of sin. Only the love of God, normally given to us through Christ, who is the Way, saves us from original sin.

63

Sin

A note on sin — even quite a lengthy one — seems to me to be necessary.

The lives of many Catholics I have known have been obsessed, made gloomy and difficult, because of the teaching they have had about sin; and very many who are no longer Catholics have abandoned their faith because — quite rightly — they have rejected a religion which was presented to them primarily as a series of rules and precepts which were then, almost inevitably, broken.

A childhood and adolescence poisoned by a sense of guilt — you only need to look around to see the results.

Believers still suffer psychologically, and therefore vitally, even when they realize intellectually the aberrations of their religious education; and because of this sort of education, unbelievers no longer recognize Christ in the Church or else have a terrible struggle when coming back to the faith.

I will now try to set forth, *not* a minimalist, but rather an almost maximalist view of sin, which, however, I hope will be more acceptable.

God is not constantly spying on you round corners, pointing his gun, ready to shoot you if you make a mistake, nor does he keep an account book. God is not the accuser, rather, 'the accuser' is a name traditionally given to Satan. It is we who, in order to get closer to God, must place ourselves on the side of truth: we must acknowledge that we are limited and therefore open to sin (as were Adam and Eve). The liturgy also says this at the beginning of each Mass: "To prepare ourselves to celebrate the sacred mysteries, let us call to mind our sins". This acknowledgement of the truth is not to accuse us but to set us free, to justify us — to use St Paul's expression. It makes us at peace with ourselves; it prepares us to receive God.

To choose truth is to side with God: then we can sin and fail but we shall be forgiven, not seven times but 'seventy times seven' (Matthew 18:22); we shall be weak, sinners, but not sinful, unworthy, condemned.

Let us remember, however — and this is not a threat but is part of the truth which is humility — let us remember that we are creatures of time, in time, and therefore we can be unfaithful to this choice. We are not 'confirmed in grace', our choices cannot yet be 'eternal'. Hence the necessity of the sacraments, of communicating and going to confession 'at least once a year'. Our choice is thus renewed and confirmed.

Sin is any act of non-love, indifference, culpable selfishness or outright hatred, towards God, our neighbour or ourselves.

The measure in which we fail to love is the measure in which we sin. You can list as many sins as you like, but they are only sins if they are acts of non-love.

That is why only subjective sins (see chapter 65) are really sins as far as our relationship with God is concerned (for example, in confession, where these are the only sins we need confess). There are, of course, degrees of non-love which lead to the distinction between venial and grave sin.

If there is only one banana in the fruit bowl and I know that the person eating with me really likes bananas and I take it, I am sinning, but only venially. If, on the other hand, I know that my neighbour has lost all his money and cannot feed his children and I do not help him although I could do so, I am committing a grave sin.

Sin, like love, is not static in each of us, but dynamic.

I like the expression 'hardness of heart' that the Bible uses so often. *Every* time we love God, our neighbour or ourselves, every time we act lovingly, our heart becomes softer. Every time we act unlovingly, our heart becomes harder. Our heart is continually changing, soft-hard-soft. Grave sins greatly harden our hearts (they also blind us).

Acts of love, of penitence, soften them.

'Mortal' sin is nothing but a grave sin which hardens our heart. The word 'mortal' presupposes that an individual is going to continue in this 'hardening' without repentance, until death; it means that he prefers non-love to love, death to life.

I think it is inaccurate to say that a person is in a state of 'mortal sin'. At the most, one could say that, objectively speaking, he has committed a mortal sin. It seems inaccurate to me because we can never know if someone has now, or at an earlier time, fulfilled all the conditions which the Church says are necessary to commit a mortal sin. There are four conditions: (1) that the act should really have been done (or not done in the case of sins of omission); (2) that it should be a serious matter (and not only thought to be so, by the individual or group; see chapter 65); (3) that the person was fully aware at the time of committing it; (4) that there was deliberate consent.

But who — except God who searches the heart — can judge if there was full awareness or deliberate consent? One knows if one has committed a grave sin, even if one is not sure if the awareness and consent were complete. That is why a Christian should never despair, but also why he should make his confession.

The year before my baptism, a friend said to me: "The essence of sin is *wasting time* — yours, God's and other people's". Seen from another angle, one could say that by sinning we remain in time, we remain slaves of time, we do not grow.

64

Sin and error

A man I greatly admire, Monsignor Carlo Colombo, once said in class — I seem to remember he was doubtful about it, but he did say it — "every error is in some sense a sin".

That really made me think. It implies that every error stems from sin; not necessarily from individual sin but from the sins of the whole of society, the sins of all men and women in time and space. Sins tend to snowball, they pollute the atmosphere; we ought also to include — but it would get too involved — original sin and the sins of the angels. So we are caught up by this evil snowball — or bits of it — and we 'go wrong'.

It is as if there were a universal conflict between good and evil, God and Satan (a war which rages in time but is already won by Christ beyond time), and, in this war, blind as we are, even if we do not sin, we often make mistakes.

Certainly, if we are responsible for subjective sin (see chapter 65), we are not necessarily responsible for objective sin, which can often be called 'error'. But, oddly enough, even in human society certain errors take on the character of sin and are punished: take for example an automobile accident when someone is killed; there is always some element of 'negligence' which is culpable — and often punished by law.

Seen from this point of view, every mistake becomes more serious: we should be much more careful, more aware of what we are doing (then, paradoxically, because it is more conscious, a 'mistake' can become 'sin'), and perhaps, in the same way, every sin of ours becomes less serious — all this should make us humbler as we realize our frailty.

65

Objective and subjective sin

The law of Friday abstinence, that is, not eating meat on a Friday, is a very old ecclesiastical law both of the Catholic Church and, with a few variations, of the Orthodox as well. like any law which is merely ecclesiastical, it is binding only when one can obey it without harming oneself or others. I use this law to illustrate the difference between objective and subjective sin because it lends itself well to this purpose.

It is Lent. I know it is Friday and I eat meat when I could very well do without. In that case I am sinning both objectively and subjectively. I believe it is Thursday but in fact it is Friday: I eat meat. I am sinning objectively but not subjectively. It is Thursday but I think it is Friday: I eat meat, and so sin subjectively but not objectively.

Only subjective sins have to be confessed. Objective ones, even if grave, are more errors than sins as far as the individual is concerned.

66

Heresies

A heresy is a doctrine which neither conforms to nor can be reconciled with the teaching of Christ as interpreted by the magisterium of the Church, but which certain people set forth as Christian doctrine.

There have been countless heresies and of many kinds. Very often the people who teach them — the heretics — do so for the best of reasons, in good faith, in order to safeguard important principles which seem to them to be threatened.

Often the proposed doctrines do not appear to be heretical at first, but the Church — as history shows us — has as it were a sixth sense for discovering them and putting the faithful on guard against them. (Unfortunately, in the course of history the cry of 'heresy' has not always been due to this sixth sense but sometimes to groundless fears — as in the case of Galileo for example — or to other less noble motives. I am not speaking of such cases here.)

I would like to mention four heresies which recur, in various forms, throughout the history of the Church and which exist here and there even today: they are those held by the Judaizers, the gnostics, the Manichees and the Pelagians.

1. *The Judaizers*. These are conservatives. The first Christians were all of Jewish origin and still followed all the dietary and other precepts of the law of Moses including circumcision. When the non-Jews began to be converted to Christianity (Cornelius in Acts 10 is the first example), the question arose as to whether they too should follow the Mosaic law. Paul maintained that Christ had liberated them from these laws. A tremendous controversy followed which resulted in the acceptance of Paul's view, expressed at the

first Ecumenical Council at Jerusalem (Acts 15). The letters of Paul to the Romans and to the Galatians deal with this problem.

The attitude underlying this heresy is constantly reappearing in a more or less disguised form in the Church: today, for example, those who oppose the reforms introduced by the Second Vatican Council and who want, say, to keep the liturgy in Latin only, are moving in the direction of this heresy.

2. *The Gnostics.* Various groups of people who, during the course of the centuries, profess fairly diverse doctrines, are classed under the generic term of 'gnostics'. This makes it hard to explain gnosticism. St John the Apostle was already attacking them in his letters. The Church has fought against certain basic errors which may be found in every type of gnosticism. The gnostics are elitists, often individualists. They 'know' they have been chosen. They have a very personal contact with God and often believe that God manifests himself through various demigods (for some of them, Christ was one of these and at the top of the hierarchy) who instruct the elect, sometimes deliberately leading everyone else astray.

Therefore the gnostics tend to underrate and oppose those institutions which are for 'everyone', for the 'common' people, or at least they feel themselves superior and not bound to the teachings given to the masses. The common people do not 'know'. In certain mediaeval forms, the Cathars, for example, gnosticism was also Manichean and the 'perfect' did not marry.

Gnosticism is rife even today: in refined forms of spirituality which deplore what they consider the coarseness, arrogance and materialism of the official Church; and in much cruder forms involving directives and messages which come straight from the divinity to the chosen few, the mass of the people being thought incapable of receiving them.

3. *Manicheism.* Manicheism has always, or nearly always, been present in Christianity. It is a doctrine of

151

oriental origin (certainly not Jewish) which separates the body from the soul and matter from spirit (see chapter 34). The Manichees are dualists. The spirit, the soul, is 'good', the body, matter, is 'bad'. These two forces, originally two Persian deities, Ormuz and Ahriman, fight for control of the world and man is in the middle.

Manicheism has many variants, even if they do not go by that name, and they are often mixed with heresies of the gnostic type. Manicheism has always been a great temptation to the Church, perhaps more to Protestants than to Catholics. St Augustine, who was a Manichee before becoming a Catholic, and who later strongly fought the Manichees, nevertheless retained many Manichean attitudes, especially in his moral doctrine. It is easy to see how a Manichean tendency could lead to repression in sexual matters.

The dogmatic teaching of the Church has always opposed Manicheism; pastoral practice, even at an official level, has often propagated this heresy.

4. *Pelagianism*. Pelagius was a saintly British monk of the fourth century who sought to reinstate human nature. He had the best of intentions and believed that it was enough to wish to imitate Christ and then to put into practice this wish in order to be saved. He thought this could be done by one's own efforts and that people fail to achieve goodness through their own laziness, slackness and ill will.

So he was a proponent of free will, an optimist, who denied the effects of original sin on human nature (see chapter 62). His theory implied that we do not need the help of God and the grace of Christ at every moment of our lives.

All those who maintain that men can and should 'go it alone' in an absolute sense — even the Church teaches that if you do not do all you can yourself, God cannot help you — all such people are modern Pelagians. The Pelagian refuses to recognize his own limitations as a human being and a creature; his great temptation is the worst of all: pride.

67

The fear of God

"*Initium sapientiae est timor Domini*". The fear of the Lord is the beginning of wisdom. We find this sentence repeated over and over again in the Bible.

Why fear God? How can one love someone whom one fears? There are three kinds of fear: the fear of the slave, the fear of the son and the fear of the lover.

The slave is afraid of being beaten — this is not the kind of fear we should have for God.

The son is afraid of being rebuked and also, perhaps, of being disinherited — this is not the kind of fear we should have for God.

The lover is afraid of displeasing the loved one, of wounding the other person — it is this fear which is the beginning of wisdom.

68

Prayer

Traditionally, there are four kinds of prayer: contrition (asking forgiveness); petition (asking for something); thanksgiving; adoration (contemplation).

Contrition — when we have done something wrong — is the acknowledgement that we have not acted right, that we would like to make amends where possible and to do the right thing in future, so we ask for help to do this.

Petition — and this is (unfortunately?) the most common sort of prayer — asks God for what we think we need. It is the kind of prayer most open to abuse and misunderstanding. When asking for something, we should think about what we really need, remembering to start with the law of Christ which is the law of love.

Prayer of thanksgiving is self-explanatory.

The Our Father includes some of all these different kinds of prayer. Each kind has its value and is suited to different moments of our lives. But the one which every Christian should aim at is the prayer of adoration: this should become our habitual form of prayer. There is a beautiful story which is told about the Curé d'Ars.

Every day, the Curé saw an old peasant standing at the back of his church, cap in hand, quite motionless and completely silent, his eyes on the tabernacle. After some days the Curé asked him why he didn't sit down, why he didn't pray.

"What are you doing there?" he asked him.

"*Je le regarde et il me regarde*" — I look at him and he looks at me — was the reply.

This is not the moment to discuss the importance of prayer and how it works. It is enough to say that the whole tradition, the saints and the magisterium have always held that without prayer we become spiritually dead. (The Church does not oblige her priests to say Mass daily, but she obliges them to recite the breviary — a compendium of prayers, taken for the most part from the Psalms — every day.) And, lastly, prayer does not 'change' God but it changes us: it opens us to him, conquers our pride, prepares us to accept his will, unites us to the Spirit who is within us.

69

Contemplatives and mystics

If God exists, and is what we have said he is, then the highest vocation for man while on earth, is to contemplate him. St Teresa of Avila tells us:

> Let nothing disturb you,
> Nothing alarm you,
> Everything passes,
> God is unchanging,
> Patience will bring you
> All that you strive for;
> He who has God
> Is lacking in nothing:
> God alone suffices.[1]

To 'contemplate' is a vocation, a calling, not a personal choice, at least for those called to a life of contemplation. But I believe that we are all called to moments of contemplation — only that we are nearly always deaf to that call.

Jesus teaches that contemplation is more important than anything we can 'do': "Martha, Martha, you are anxious and troubled about many things; one thing is needful. Mary has chosen the good portion, which shall not be taken away from her" (Luke 10:41-42).

People have very little understanding of this; for them contemplatives are egocentric, egotistical people seeking a life of personal tranquillity and comfortable idleness. But if one understands the doctrine of the Communion of Saints (see chapter 55) one understands that convents and monasteries of contemplative monks and nuns are 'powerhouses of grace' as Thomas Merton calls them. The contemplative who gives himself and his whole life to God in imitation of Christ, tends to become perfectly obedient and so is a perfect human instrument in the hands of God. He does not 'do', (God does not particularly need men to 'do' things for him) he just 'is' (see chapter 46).

It is very surprising for those who do not know these things, and delightful for those who do, to find that contemplatives — who are usually allowed few visitors — are not only full of peace but extraordinarily and contagiously joyful.

There is a great difference between a contemplative and a mystic. Contemplatives are those who give themselves to God; God calls them and they answer the call. Mystics are those whom God 'takes'. Contemplatives feel called to contemplation; they know that they have to dedicate their lives to God in silence and prayer. (Many religious orders are 'contemplative': Carthusians, Trappists, Carmelites, etc.). Mystics, on the other hand, are those on whom God 'lays his hand', whom God 'takes', who receive a supernatural experience (a vision, a sensation, a feeling . . .), a mystical experience in fact. (St Paul on the road to Damascus had a mystical experience as did St Francis of Assisi at the time of his conversion, and the same applies to many other saints; see especially the works of St John of the Cross and St Teresa of Avila.)

Contemplatives can pass their whole lives without having a supernatural experience of God, a 'mystical' experience. Certainly, contemplatievs are often mystics.

The mystical tradition, like the contemplative, is very little known to the great majority of Catholics, yet these traditions are of the utmost importance in the building of the Body of Christ.

The great Catholic mystics are fairly numerous: we have some of the Fathers of the Church; the English mystics of the fourteenth century in particular (the anonymous *Cloud of Unknowing* from that period is extraordinarily beautiful); the German mystics of the Rhine, of roughly the same period: Ruysbroek, Eckhart, Suso, Tauler; the Spaniards from Lull to St Teresa of Avila and St John of the Cross; the Italian Saints Catherine of Genoa and Siena, Angela of Foligno, Francis and so on.

There are also great non-Christian mystics, Hallaj and Rabia among the Moslems, certain of the Jewish Hassidim and many Orientals. There are very interesting studies comparing the various traditions.

Every Christian should learn to 'contemplate' (see chapter 68) but God makes a mystic of whom he wills.

1. Nada te turbe, / nada te espante, / todo se pasa, / Dios no se muda, / la paciencia / todo lo alcanza; / quien a Dios tiene / nada le falta: / solo Dios basta.

70

Christianity and other religions or "why have missionaries?"

The relationship between Christianity and other faiths is a difficult subject to treat briefly these days because there are so many new lines of thought to follow, and so much is being said intelligently on the matter.[1]

In an outline of Christianity as this book presents, one can include — as I have tried to show — many aspects of different religions. Many new openings are being explored, with mutual wariness but also, fortunately, with joyful trepidation.

God has certainly manifested himself "in many and various ways" to the whole of mankind, as the beginning of the Letter to the Hebrews tells us; and as we have seen, every individual who follows his own religion, that is, who follows the good and true insofar as he knows it — with the firm desire always to know more and to do better — will be 'saved' (see chapter 26). The Church, however, holds that Christianity, and in particular the Roman Catholic version, is the 'true' religion, and wants all men to be part of it.

Why then should a non-Christian, who can be 'saved' even if he remains outside the Church, become a Christian? And why should a Christian bother to convert others to Christianity? Why have missionaries? (I am leaving aside the historical and social polemics about how constructively or unconstructively missions have functioned — my concern is strictly theological.)

The general answer to all these questions is simple. If, in order to give glory to God — which is the reason for creation (see chapter 30) — it is necessary to manifest

Christ, to proclaim and preach Christ, this can only be done by being a Christian.

We witness Christ explicitly by being part of his visible Mystical Body, the Church, by eating his Eucharistic Body and by participating in the sacraments.[2]

In theory — though not necessarily in practice — the Christian should be able to love 'better'. Having Christ, who is love in human form, as model, and, what is more, partaking of his Body and Blood in the sacraments, and being a member of his Body which is the Church, love should be an integral part of the Christian's life, the basis of his world view and the mainspring of his actions.

We are saying that the individual Christian could and should love more and love better, *not* that historically this has actually happened; rather history more often indicates the opposite; this surprises and scandalizes people; it can only be explained if we take into consideration human freedom and its abuse.

Where there is a greater possibility of good, there is also a greater possibility of evil (splitting the atom leads to incredibly cheap energy *and* to Hiroshima.) Graham Greene in his novels shows the many contradictions which arise out of the encounter and clash between grace and human freedom in the individual.[3]

Similarly — but this requires closer study — only by being a part of the visible Body can one, on this earth at least, be a part of the Communion of Saints (see chapter 55) and so participate in the redeeming of the world and make up "what is lacking in Christ's afflictions for the sake of his body, that is, the Church", as St Paul says (Colossians 1 : 24). The Church must always be missionary, proclaiming Christ and carrying on the work of salvation. But this does not give prerogatives or personal advantages to the individual Christian, rather it is a position fraught with risks and dangers. The advantages are only those of a lover who serves his beloved (and those are no small advantages for a lover). A Christian is above all a servant, servant of God and of his neighbour. The Pope's most beautiful title has always seemed to me to be 'Servus servorum Dei', the Servant of the servants of God.

1. See the writings of Raymond Panikkar and particularly *The Unknown Christ of Hinduism*, Darton, Longman and Todd, 1964.

2. In this connection it would be interesting to study the case of Simone Weil, a Jew who believed in Christianity, but who never asked for baptism — and so was deprived of the Eucharist, in which she fervently believed — out of solidarity with her people, then suffering under Hitler's persecution.

The problem raised here is this: is it possible to refuse to receive the 'visible' Body of Christ out of love? If the answer is yes, then Simone Weil was right. In any case, these are choices which only a saint can make.

3. See, e.g., *The Power and the Glory*, *The Heart of the Matter* and *The End of the Affair*, Penguin Books.

Conclusion

"But there are also many other things which Jesus did; were every one of them to be written, I suppose that the world itself could not contain the books that would be written", St John tells us at the end of his Gospel (21 : 25).

And I, re-reading what I have written, see many omissions. I justify myself by recalling that I only set out to write 'notes'.

There are so many important matters which I have not even mentioned. Such as the relationship between Christianity and the social and political problems of today, or the problems of morality and ethics, on which I would have much to say. I say very little about the sacraments, the Eucharist for example — and these are enormous gaps. Again, thinking it over more, I would certainly find other essential parts of Christianity which I have said nothing about (I could have said so much, for example, on the theological virtues of faith, hope and charity). But enough, that will be for another time — perhaps. Wittgenstein, in the preface to the *Tractatus Logico-Philosophicus*, says:

> This book will perhaps only be understood by those who have themselves already thought the thoughts which are expressed in it — or similar thoughts. It is therefore not a text-book. Its object would be attained if there were one person who read it with understanding and to whom it afforded pleasure.[1]

I make his words my own, adding just two more: joy and peace.

---

1. Ludwig Wittgenstien, *Tractatus Logico-Philosophicus*, Kegan Paul, 1933, p. 27.

162